Resolution

Resolution

The Story of Captain Cook's
Second Voyage of Discovery

Peter Aughton

Cold Spring Press

Cold Spring Press
P.O. Box 284
Cold Spring Harbor, NY 11724
E-mail: Jopenroad@aol.com

First published in Great Britain in 2004
by Weidenfeld & Nicolson
in association with Windrush Press

Printed in the United States of America

To Isobel Ellen

Contents

Maps

Preface

The year was 1771. The place was Hinchinbrook, the Huntingdon seat of the fourth Earl of Sandwich, First Lord of the Admiralty, and the occasion was a reception given by Lord Sandwich. The main guests were three explorers who had recently returned to England with their ship, the *Endeavour*, after making a remarkable voyage of discovery in the Pacific Ocean. The three were Captain James Cook, Mr Joseph Banks and Dr Daniel Solander.

James Cook had mapped and charted the North and South Islands of New Zealand, he had discovered fertile new lands on the east coast of New Holland and he had charted the coast from nearly 40° S as far as 10° from the Equator. The expedition had observed the transit of the planet Venus across the face of the Sun and the Royal Society was using the results to calculate the distance from the Earth to the Sun. Cook had sailed his ship through the Straits of Torres and had reached home via Indonesia and the Cape of Good Hope. On his return journey he had suffered terrible casualties crossing the Indian Ocean, but the remarkable thing was that the three-year voyage had been virtually free of the scourge of scurvy. Cook had proved that long voyages to the southern oceans were perfectly possible and no sooner had the *Endeavour* returned to England than there was talk of a second voyage. There was no shortage of volunteers to undertake three years of danger and hardship on the far side of the globe.

The voyage made a great impact on public opinion and it had

caught the imagination of English society. Joseph Banks and his Swedish friend Dr Daniel Solander had accompanied Captain Cook on this great voyage around the world. The two scientists had returned with the most comprehensive collection ever made of previously unknown flora and fauna from the southern hemisphere.

Joseph Banks was presented to King George III, first at St James's Palace and a second time at Richmond. He was well connected, wealthy and aristocratic. He could enthuse about his voyage to the listeners at court, to tell them of the great discoveries in the South Seas and to obtain royal support for the proposed new voyage to the Pacific Ocean. His efforts and his thousands of botanical specimens were greatly appreciated by the scientific community and he was lionised by the Royal Society. There were also his paintings and drawings, made by the deceased artists Alexander Buchan and Sydney Parkinson, artists whom he himself had sponsored from his own private means. The artists had left a valuable record of the voyage of the *Endeavour*. It was very near the truth to say that it was entirely due to Joseph Banks that the world had this unique pictorial record.

It was not surprising that the public came to call the recent voyage of discovery 'Joseph Banks's Voyage'. It was not that he deliberately tried to overshadow the achievements of James Cook: he was doing no more than enthusing about his experiences and promoting the great success of the voyage to London society. It can be argued that without the enthusiasm and publicity given by Joseph Banks, the voyage would not have had such a great impact on the public. James Cook was relegated to no more than the chauffeur who had driven the famous Joseph Banks with his entourage and menagerie around the world. When the Swedish botanist Carl Linnaeus heard about the many new specimens from New South Wales, he was so impressed that he proposed calling the new land by the ridiculous name of 'Banksia'.

It was not all roses, however, for Joseph Banks. When he left England in 1768, he was engaged to Miss Harriet Blosset. The last time he saw her before his departure was at the opera when he did not have the nerve to tell her that he was leaving for the ends of the earth on the morrow. In 1771, when at last the *Endeavour* landed back in England after a three-year voyage, Joseph made no effort whatsoever to contact his betrothed. London society knew that Harriet had been waiting three years for his return; a letter from Lady Mary Coke, a friend of Miss Blosset, mentions the embroidered waistcoats she had been making for him whilst he was sailing around the world. Daines Barrington, one of Banks's acquaintances, wrote two letters to his friend Thomas Pennant describing the affair. We find that eventually Joseph Banks and Harriet Blosset did meet again. All through the night they talked about their feelings for each other, from ten in the evening until ten in the morning. Joseph Banks offered to marry her. Harriet suspected, however, that his heart was not in the marriage and she suggested they wait a fortnight to see if he was still of the same mind. A letter from Daines Barrington explains the facts as he heard them and what happened next:

> I have receiv'd at this place a most particular account from a Lady of what hath pass'd between Mr Banks & Miss Blosset who strongly confirms that the former made the most explicit declaration.
>
> What think you of the following facts?
>
> Mr Banks had an interview with her in London which lasted from ten O'clock at Night to ten the next Morning during which he said he was ready to marry her immediately.
>
> Miss Blosset however would not catch at this proposal but told him if he was of the same mind a fortnight hence, she would gladly attend him to church. Three or four days after which he wrote her a letter desiring to be off.
>
> Mr Tunstall writes me word that Mr Banks and Dr Solander mean to fall plump from the Cape of Good Hope upon 70 Degs of Southern Latitude
>
> Ever Yrs
> D: B:
>
> P.S. Mr Banks in this conversation said he had acted by the advice of a friend & hence the Blossets blame Solander as I before inform'd you.[1]

The postscript implies that Banks had consulted his friend Daniel Solander, but it seems harsh to lay any blame in that quarter. The rest of society clearly thought that Banks's behaviour was very shameful and even his snobbish and aristocratic mother, who never approved of the Blossets in the first place, thought he was at fault over the way he had treated his intended.

The other item of interest in Barrington's letter refers to the plans for a further voyage. Banks and Solander were preparing to sail south from the Cape of Good Hope. In the mind of Joseph Banks, the planning of the next voyage clearly took priority over any thoughts of tying the matrimonial knot. He also assumed that he would be in command of the next expedition. It would be he, not James Cook, who would give the orders as the ship sailed round the world. It would be he, Joseph Banks, who would ensure that the expedition would serve the needs of natural history. It would be he who would decide where and when the ship would sail, and where and when to land and botanise.

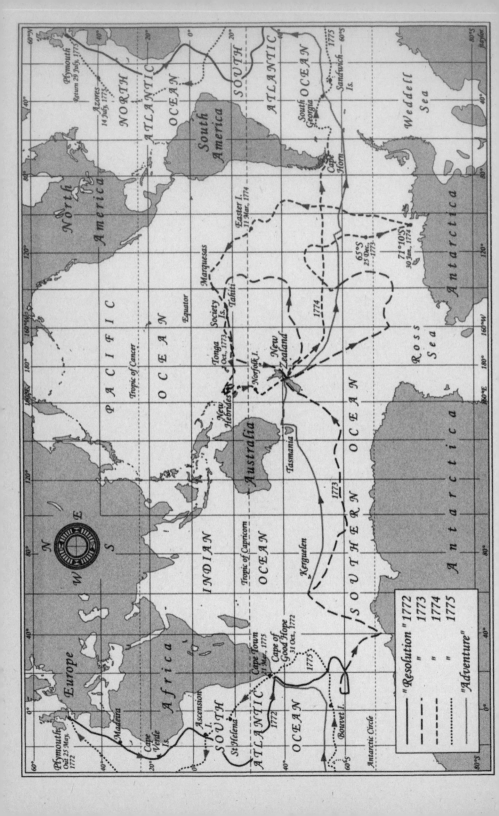

ONE

London and Yorkshire

Their hands outstretched in yearning for the further shore
Aeneid, II, 314

Charles Burney was a doctor of music and the most sought-after music teacher in London. The Burneys were a family of great artistic, literary and musical talents. Charles's nineteen-year-old daughter Fanny kept a diary and had ambitions to become a novelist, but the famous meeting with Dr Samuel Johnson which helped to launch her career lay in the future. Fanny's brother James Burney was in the Royal Navy: he was a young man of twenty-one who had recently returned from Bombay on the East Indiaman *Greenwich*. In spite of his youth, young Burney already had more than ten years' service with the Navy. He arrived home to find the country afire with the exploits and discoveries made by the *Endeavour* in the southern seas. He longed to sail the Pacific himself if only the opportunity would present itself. He was prepared to sign up at any cost and he knew that his well-connected father was the best person to champion his cause.

Fanny's diary tells us how Dr Burney first made the acquaintance of Lord Sandwich. Her brother was not the only person who hoped to gain from Charles Burney's connections in high places:

My father has had a happy opportunity of extremely obliging Dr. Hawkesworth. During his stay in Norfolk, he waited upon Lord Orford, who has always been particularly friendly to him. He there, among others, met with Lord Sandwich. His Lordship was speaking of the late voyage round the world and mentioned his having the papers of it in his possession, for he is the first Lord of the Admiralty; and said that they were not arranged, but mere rough draughts, and that he should be much obliged to anyone who could recommend a proper person to write the voyage.[2]

It just so happened that Dr Burney *was* in a position to recommend a proper person to write the official account of the voyage. He seemed to have the ability to obtain any favour for any person of his acquaintance. Fanny did not seem to approve of the choice, but she thought the world of her father.

My father directly named Dr. Hawkesworth, and his Lordship did him the honour to accept his recommendation. The Doctor waited upon Lord Sandwich, and they both returned my father particular thanks for their meeting. Yet I cannot but be amazed, that a man of Sandwich's power, etc., should be so ignorant of men of earning and merit, as to apply to an almost stranger for recommendation. Pity! Pity! That those only should be sensible of who cannot reward worth![3]

The notebooks and journals from the *Endeavour* voyage were subsequently given on loan to John Hawkesworth, who had the enviable task of writing the official account of the great voyage of discovery. Hawkesworth was an experienced journalist and he was well qualified in naval matters. He was acquainted with Samuel Johnson and he could write so well in the ponderous but fashionable Johnsonian style that his anonymous pieces were sometimes mistaken for Johnson's work. There was every reason to suppose that Hawkesworth would make a good job of his assignment, but his task was made more onerous by the fact that his account was expected to include the other English voyages into the Pacific Ocean prior to the *Endeavour*, namely those of Byron, Wallis and Carteret. The account of four circumnavigations caused his account to run to three sizeable volumes.

The remarkable Charles Burney pulled off yet another *coup* when he persuaded Captain Cook to accept an invitation to dine at the Burney household in Queen Square. At this time, the Burneys' London residence was a fashionable Georgian house in Bloomsbury, at the edge of the residential developments and with vistas across the open fields to Hampstead and Highgate. In 1774 the Burneys moved to the house which had been occupied by the great scientist Sir Isaac Newton fifty years earlier, but the move to Leicester Fields was still a few years in the future. The house was not as crowded as a British man o' war, but it was densely populated for a Bloomsbury household. Dr and Mrs Burney had both been widowed. Charles Burney brought six children with him from his first marriage, including Fanny and also James when he was at home. Elizabeth Burney was the widow of Stephen Allen and she brought with her three Allen children. Charles and Elizabeth were also blessed with two younger children from their own marriage, making a total of eleven children in the household. In such a numerous family there must have been plenty of sibling jealousy, heated exchanges and adolescent tantrums, but by and large the children lived very happily together, the older children helping and supporting younger brothers and sisters. In fact, the Burney household was a marvellous and stimulating environment for young people – not least because of the number of interesting visitors that Dr Burney brought home to meet his family.

James Cook arrived at the Burney household. He was not as relaxed as Joseph Banks would have been in such erudite company and Fanny noted in her memoirs that 'this truly great man appeared to be full of sense and thought; well-mannered and perfectly unpretending; but studiously wrapped up in his own purposes and pursuits; and apparently under a pressure of mental fatigue when called upon to speak, or stimulated to deliberate, upon any other ... [purpose or pursuit]'. Cook was a confident and eloquent enough man at home, in his own environment on board his ship, and with his naval superiors and friends such as Joseph Banks and Daniel Solander from the scientific community. However, the literary and artistic world of the Burneys was very different from his own upbringing and it was quite unfamiliar to him. His impassive silence and deep meditation were excellent qualities for the commander of one of His Majesty's ships but he was out of his depth with the light-hearted chat and gossipy social functions of this sector of London society.

It was only a minor problem, for Charles Burney knew how to put his guest at ease. He produced a volume of the recently published *Voyage Autour du Monde* by the French navigator Louis Antoine de Bougainville. This cannot have been the first time that Cook had seen the account of Bougainville's voyage – he would have devoured the book as soon as he could lay his hands on it – but it brought the conversation round to a topic on which he could converse well and on which he could contribute more than anybody else present. Charles Burney asked James Cook how his route around the world compared to that of Bougainville. Cook relaxed; he was now in his element. He produced a pencil from his pocket book. He traced the track of the *Endeavour* across the North and South Atlantic, around Cape Horn and across the South Pacific to Tahiti. He showed the circuitous route from Tahiti to New Zealand and he traced the circumnavigation of both the North and South Islands in a part of the Pacific that appeared as a complete blank on Bougainville's map. In another blank space he showed the passage to New South Wales and the charting of the east coast of New Holland right up to Cape York. He showed the route through the Indonesian islands to Batavia, followed by the terrible crossing of the Indian Ocean where many of his crew died. He showed the landing at Cape Town and the final leg of the voyage around Africa, Portugal, the Bay of Biscay and back to the English Channel.

Dr Burney often talked to his friends about the incident: '[He] ... said he would trace the route, which he did in so clear and scientific a manner, that I would not take 50 pounds for the book. The pencil marks having been fixed by skim milk, will always be visible.' So highly did Charles Burney value the *Voyage Autour du Monde* that it eventually found its way into the British Museum Library where it was retained for posterity. Dr Burney seems to have been under the mistaken impression that the English and French navigators had actually met each other where their tracks crossed and that there had been a cool exchange between them. However, he was actually confusing the incident with a meeting between Bougainville's ship *Boudeuse* and Carteret's *Swallow* in February 1769.

A question which few seemed to ask was why, when the *Endeavour* seemed to have left nothing to discover in the southern hemisphere, was everybody talking about another voyage so soon after her return? Very few people still believed in the existence of the great southern continent, but it was just possible that more habitable land existed at high latitudes in the south. Cook had sailed to a latitude of nearly 50° S when he rounded the South Island of New Zealand. He had penetrated to nearly 60° S when he rounded Cape Horn, but this was in well-charted waters and no new discoveries were expected in that vicinity.

Apart from New Zealand and Cape Horn, the rest of the voyage had been conducted in latitudes of less than 40°.

In the northern hemisphere, the fortieth parallel runs through Turkey, Greece, the foot of Italy and the centre of Spain. The British mainland, apart from a tiny fraction of Cornwall, is all north of latitude 50°. Norway, Sweden and Finland touch the Arctic Circle. In America the forty-ninth parallel had yet to be recognized as an international boundary. There were few settlements north of this line, but many of the American Colonies were north of the fortieth parallel. It was well known that land existed in America as far north as the Arctic Circle and probably beyond. Land and life obviously flourished at high latitudes in the north, so why not in the south? Where was the great landmass in the south to balance the land in the north? It seemed a reasonable question. Cook himself had no doubt that the *Terra Australis Incognita* did not exist, certainly not in the idealised form put forward by Alexander Dalrymple and his supporters. However, he did agree that there could be land in the high latitudes and he wanted to be the man to explore these latitudes to establish the facts one way or another.

There were other reasons for the new expedition. It must be remembered that the *Endeavour* was by no means the first British expedition to explore the southern seas. It was simply the most successful. For more than a decade, the British government had been sending vessels to the Pacific Ocean and every voyage had been followed by another voyage leaving soon after the previous one had returned. Byron's expedition lasted from 1764 to 1766; he was followed by Wallis and Carteret, who left England together in 1766, returning in 1768 and 1769 respectively. James Cook's *Endeavour* voyage lasted from 1768 to 1771. The Admiralty was always in favour of making another voyage of discovery, and even more so after the success of the *Endeavour*. There was still plenty of the great southern ocean that had never been explored and it was necessary for the British to consolidate their claims to the discoveries made by Cook and his crew.

Cook's success in conquering scurvy was another major factor. The methods of prevention were reasonably well established and this meant that new expeditions no longer had to face this terrible disease. There was also the question of finding the longitude at sea. Cook, with the assistance of his deceased astronomer Charles Green, had known at all

times, to within a few nautical miles, whereabouts he was on the surface
of the earth. The science of navigation had moved on in the three years
he had been away. John Harrison's marine chronometer had proved a
great success and other clockmakers had successfully copied his
designs. The number of marine chronometers could still be counted on
one hand, but unlike Harrison's number four, they were not unique
and they could now be spared for exploration. Cook still looked upon
the newfangled technology with a certain degree of suspicion, but he
was sufficiently open-minded to give it a trial.

The route and the details of the new expedition were still under
discussion, but the Admiralty was happy to let Cook go ahead with
the choice of his own ship. He wanted a ship of the same construction
as the *Endeavour* and it didn't take him long to find one. He wanted two
ships for the voyage, so that if he had a repetition of the *Endeavour*'s
disaster on the Great Barrier Reef, he could at least rescue his crew. In
November 1771 he was negotiating with William Hammond of Hull to
purchase two ships, the *Marquis of Granby* and the *Marquis of Rockingham*,
of 450 and 336 tons respectively. They had been built in the Fishburn
Yard at Whitby. Here we see the conservative side of James Cook.
Faster, larger and more comfortable ships were available, but he made
no effort to look beyond the Whitby yard. He felt no cause to do so.
The *Endeavour* had proved herself on his latest voyage: she had the
carrying capacity and the manœuvrability needed for a voyage of
exploration. She lost a little in speed and she rolled hard in heavy
weather, but she had a shallow draught for exploring coastal waters
and she could ride out any storm the Pacific could throw at her. Most
important, the Whitby collier was also the ship which Cook knew best,
the ship in which he had sailed the North Sea in his youth. He knew
exactly what she was capable of and exactly how she would handle, and
he saw no point in choosing any other design of ship.

The *Marquis of Granby* went to the Deptford yard on the Thames for
refitting and the *Marquis of Rockingham* to Woolwich. The *Marquis of
Granby* was to be refitted to carry twelve guns and a complement of 120
men. The *Marquis of Rockingham* was to carry ten guns and eighty men.
The ships would be renamed and registered as the sloops *Drake* and
Raleigh. Cook would be captain of the *Drake* and a Devonshire man,
Tobias Furneaux, was appointed as commander of the *Raleigh*.

In December, Cook asked for three weeks' leave of absence to visit his father and other relatives in Yorkshire. The application was granted and he decided to take his wife Elizabeth with him: it made a pleasant interlude and a break between the multitudinous preparations needed for the forthcoming voyage. The visit was slightly marred by the fact that the season was the middle of winter, but this was offset by the nostalgic experience of Christmas in his home county. There was another advantage of a winter visit. The London air was notoriously dirty. The smoke from the burning of sea coal, which Cook himself had helped to transport in an earlier life, cast a smog over the whole city. The problem was at its worst in the cold weather and particularly around Christmas, when the fog lay heavy in the Thames basin. The smoke in the West End was bad enough, but in the East End, where the Cook family lived, it was even worse. To a man who loved the northern moors and the open horizons of the sea it would be a relief to be free of the smoky London air for a few weeks.

At this point in time, James and Elizabeth Cook had four children. The two oldest children, James junior and Nathaniel, were growing lads of nine and eight years respectively. In common with most families of the time, James and Elizabeth also had their tragedies. Their daughter Elizabeth was just four when James Cook was returning from the Pacific. She would have been a delightful child to a father who had been three years away from home, but she died just two months before the *Endeavour* docked in England. Cook never knew his fourth child, Joseph, who was born and died in the first year of the *Endeavour* voyage. It seems that the two surviving children, James and Nathaniel, were old enough to be left in the care of friends or neighbours, so the visit to Yorkshire must have been pure delight to Elizabeth Cook, who, after three long years waiting for her husband to return, had the rare satisfaction of his full attention for three whole weeks.

Had he travelled on his own, James Cook might have gone by sea and relived part of his youth sailing the North Sea coast, but a sea voyage would have been a miserable journey for Elizabeth in the cold and short December days and they chose instead to journey along the Great North Road. It was a long journey from the Thames to the Tees, almost the full length of England. There is a slight irony in the fact that for Cook's sea voyages we have a day-to-day record of events, but when it comes to details of his visits home we can only speculate, due to incomplete data. The bustle of the great city was left behind as the two of them journeyed out into the English countryside. Each day they travelled further northwards, probably by stage, on the road to the North Riding of Yorkshire.

This was the first time that Elizabeth had travelled so far from London. The accents broadened the further north they travelled, but this was no problem to the Essex-born Elizabeth as long as she had her husband to help with the local dialects. The towns and villages of the Great North Road were used to meeting travellers, but the great majority of people in the eighteenth century were not well travelled: they considered the nearest market town to be a long journey. Few, if any, of those they met on the road would have known that this man was the greatest traveller and explorer of the age.

At last they were north of York and journeying across the Yorkshire moors until the Cleveland Hills appeared on the horizon and the familiar outline of Roseberry Topping proclaimed that James Cook was back in the land of his birth. The cottage at Great Ayton which had been bought and lived in by Cook's parents was still standing, but it was no longer occupied by either of them. Cook's mother, Grace, had been dead for six years. His father, James Cook Senior, was still alive at the age of seventy-seven but was living with his daughter, Margaret Fleck, a fisherman's wife who lived in the coastal village of Redcar. Cook nevertheless decided to spend some time at Great Ayton. This was partly out of sentiment, but he also arranged to meet a retired Commodore, William Wilson, who had served in the East India Company and was himself an explorer of some repute. Commodore Wilson had discovered the Pitt Passage that lay between the Moluccas and New Guinea and that served as an alternative route to China, avoiding the straits of Singapore. William Wilson's wife was the sister of George Jackson, the secretary to the Admiralty. James Cook and William Wilson formed a close friendship in the short time they were together. They had much in common and it made the brief visit to Great Ayton all the more pleasant and satisfying.

The next port of call was Redcar, where Cook witnessed again the familiar pounding of the North Sea as it eroded the cliffs of the Yorkshire coast. At Redcar there was a family reunion. Much as Grace Cook was sorely missed, we can but imagine the pride of James Cook Senior, who had lived to see his son return from the southern hemisphere as the nation's most celebrated explorer. Few men, particularly in the humble situation of Cook's father, have the good fortune to live long enough to see their sons achieve so much. It seems certain that the Cook family celebrated Christmas together in the humble fisherman's cottage at Redcar.

We have one reliable account of Cook's visit to Yorkshire. He wrote a letter to Captain William Hammond of Hull, the shipping merchant from whom he had negotiated the purchase of the two ships for his coming voyage. His original plan was to visit Hull, but his itinerary did not give him sufficient time:

I am sorry to acquaint you that it is now out of my power to meet you at Whitby, nor will it be convenient for me to return by way of Hull as I had resolved upon three days ago. Mrs Cook being but a bad traveler, I was prevailed upon to lay that route aside on account of the reported badness of the roads and therefore took horse on Tuesday morning, and rode over to Whitby, and returned yesterday. Your friends at that place expect to see you every day. I have only myself to blame for not having the pleasure of meeting you there. I am informed by letter from Lieut Cooper that the Admiralty have altered the names of the Ships from *Drake* to *Resolution*, and *Raleigh* to *Adventurer* which, in my opinion, are much properer than the former. I set out for London to morrow morning, shall only stop a day or two at York.[4]

The visit on horseback to Whitby is thus well enough authenticated. The prestige of Cook in his home county was so high that a certain folklore has emerged around his deeds and his character, but even if the accounts are distorted by sentiment, they are as close to the truth as we are likely to get. It was the last day of 1771 and the men of Whitby, so proud of the achievements of their own ship the *Endeavour*, rode out on horseback to greet the explorer at Swarthowe Cross on the edge of the moors. Everybody in Whitby wanted to claim an acquaintance with the great explorer, but some had stronger claims than others and Cook was entertained by his old employer John Walker. He visited his old lodgings in the Walker household, where, according to the legend, he had spent many solitary hours getting to grips with the mathematics of navigation. Mary Prowd, the elderly housekeeper, had no qualms about showing her emotions. She threw her arms around him and cried 'Oh honey James! How glad I is to see thee!' The visit to Yorkshire was full of moving and emotional reunions. But all too soon, in the first week of the new year, James and Elizabeth had to return to their duties and responsibilities in London. They intended to stay a few days in York, where the sight of the walled city with its ancient streets and the grandeur of the minster would be a moving new experience for Elizabeth.

In Yorkshire and back in London, there was much talk of the new expedition. James Boswell recorded a conversation with Samuel Johnson regarding the renaming of the two ships for the second time:

> A gentleman having come in who was to go as a mate in the ship along with Mr Banks and Dr Solander, Dr Johnson asked what were the names of the ships destined for the expedition. The gentleman answered, they were once to be called the *Drake* and *Ralegh* but now they were to be called the *Resolution* and the *Adventure*.
>
> JOHNSON: 'Much better, for had the *Ralegh* returned without going round the world it would have been ridiculous. To give them the names of the *Drake* and the *Ralegh* was laying a trap for satire.'[5]

It is curious that Johnson seemed to think that it was Raleigh and not Drake who sailed around the world – but this is probably no more than a slip of the pen on Boswell's part. The reason given by the Admiralty for renaming the ships was that Drake and Raleigh were still remembered by the Spanish as pirates and plunderers of the Spanish Main. It was obvious that two ships with these names in the Pacific Ocean would meet nothing but anger if they happened to encounter the Spanish. Boswell's next passage is of greater interest:

> BOSWELL: 'Had you not some desire to go upon this expedition, Sir?'
>
> JOHNSON: 'Why yes, but I soon laid it aside. Sir, there is very little of intellectual, in the course. Besides, I see but at a small distance. So it was not worth my while to go to see birds fly, which I should not have seen fly, and fishes swim which I should not of seen swim.'[6]

How Johnson could claim that 'there is very little of intellectual, in the course' is a complete mystery. When the *Endeavour* brought back more scientific knowledge of the southern hemisphere than any other previous voyage, Johnson claimed that there were plenty of insects in England already without importing even more. How Johnson could possibly contemplate a voyage around the world is an even greater mystery. Was it not the great Samuel Johnson who said in 1759 that 'No man will be a sailor who has contrivance enough to get himself into jail; for being in a ship is being in jail, with the chance of being drowned'? Nothing could be more ridiculous than the thought of Dr Johnson on board one of Cook's ships, but we must remember that Johnson loved to play devil's advocate and all his remarks must be taken tongue in cheek. The conversation then turned to a hare-brained scheme of the good doctor's to purchase the remote island of St Kilda; the outermost of the Outer Hebrides; no doubt motivated by the very laudable motive of improving the hard life of the resident population.

During Cook's absence in Yorkshire, Joseph Banks had been very active. Joseph was going to amaze the world with his new voyage. His plan was not merely to explore to the south of the Cape of Good Hope, but to sail as far as the South Pole! 'O how Glorious would it be to set my heel upon the Pole! And turn myself round 360° in a second,' he declared. The whole scientific community of Europe was informed of the great deeds he intended to achieve. Through his contacts with the Royal Society, he was communicating with the scientific communities of France, Holland, Germany, Switzerland and Sweden. Money was no problem to a man of his means: he was prepared to use his own fortune to sponsor the venture. He organised the striking of a medal to be distributed throughout the Pacific; it depicted the two ships and carried the date 1772 to stake the claim of the British to their discoveries. The medal was struck by the Birmingham financier Matthew Boulton at his Soho works, famous for the development of James Watt's marvellous steam engine, the prime mover of the industrial revolution. An exchange of letters took place between Soho in London and Soho in Birmingham.

Joseph Banks began to recruit his scientific staff. It went without saying that Dr Daniel Solander would sail again. He persuaded the talented Dr James Lind of Edinburgh to join his party as astronomer – not as the official astronomer, for that choice was the prerogative of the Admiralty, but Lind was talented in many sciences and would be a

great asset to the expedition. He even approached Joseph Priestley
with a request to join him but the great scientist did not have the time
or the inclination to spend three years travelling around the world.
Banks did manage to recruit the talented artist John Zoffany to paint
the new landscapes and scenery that they were to discover. He recruited
others to assist Zoffany and his complement began to grow. The other
arts must not be ignored and two horn players were recruited; their
function was to help produce a civilised atmosphere in the great cabin
on the relaxed summer evenings aboard the ship.

The Banks entourage soon grew to double figures then to fifteen and
then to a complement of seventeen. There was going to be a problem
of space to accommodate them all on the *Resolution*, but this was not a
serious problem to a man of Joseph Banks's means. The *Resolution* would
be modified to provide additional accommodation. The narrow-minded
Navy board refused to allow Mr Banks's wonderful alterations and
improvements, but this, too, was a minor problem to a man with Joseph
Banks's connections. He went straight to the top and got the approval
of Lord Sandwich for his plans.

The carpenters set to work on the *Resolution*. First, the waist of the
ship was built higher. Then a whole new poop deck was added to the
structure. On top of this, a raised poop or roundhouse was constructed
for the use of the captain – the captain's cabin having already been
commandeered for the use of the Banks party. The yard at Deptford
became one of the minor sights of London as society came from the
West End to stare at the wonderful ship that Mr Banks was creating
for his new voyage around the world. Everybody knew that Mr Banks
was an experienced sailor and his nautical knowledge was being used
to improve the *Resolution* and to provide extra comfort for the long
voyage to come. On 2 May the French ambassador was entertained on
board with other important personages. The First Lord of the Admiralty,
the inventor of the sandwich, came to see the improvements.

James Cook was still on good terms with Joseph Banks and he wanted
the naturalist to sail with him. He thought that the *Resolution* could
cope with the reconstruction and he made no objections to the changes.
But Joseph Banks had taken over the expedition and there seemed to
be very little that Cook could do about it. It was to be Banks's voyage
and he was to be the man in charge. He would make the important

decisions of where to go and when to land, with Cook as little more than the master of the ship carrying out his orders. The captain's quarters and the great cabin of the ship had been taken over by Joseph Banks's entourage, while the captain had been relegated to a round hut built on top of the grand new poop deck.

Resolution and Adventure

... The freshly caulked ship floats
... already the sail invites the wind.

Aeneid, IV, 398, 417

Tobias Furneaux was given orders to proceed to Plymouth with his ship the *Adventure*. At the same time, the *Resolution* was launched into the Thames with her new luxury accommodation, under the direction of Robert Cooper, who had been chosen as her first lieutenant. It was the morning of 10 May 1772 and the restructured ship set off with a light breeze from the north. The wind swung round to the east and the ship began to work her way down river, tacking into the wind. The floating pleasure palace proceeded gingerly down the river, but it was soon very obvious that something was wrong. The *Resolution* was cumbersome and unhappy. The ship was described as 'crank', which meant that she leaned too much to one side when the topsails were set. Sailing the ship was slow work and it took four whole days to reach the mouth of the Thames at the Nore, off Sheerness. There was no escaping the fact that she handled atrociously; in fact, she handled so badly that they dared not take her any further into the open sea.

Mr Banks knew nothing about centres of gravity and centres of buoyancy: it was up to others to get such things right for him. The ship was so top-heavy that she threatened to capsize every time they set the topsails. The pilot and first lieutenant shook their heads and declared her to be an 'exceeding dangerous and unsafe ship'. Charles Clerke, the second lieutenant, was more outspoken and had no qualms about voicing his opinion directly to Joseph Banks: 'By God I'll go to Sea in a Grog Tub, if desired, or in the *Resolution* as soon as you please;

but I must say I think her by far the most unsafe ship I ever saw or
heard of.' Joseph Banks had been given enough rope and he had hanged
himself – or at least he had hanged his cause. Cook gave his own
summing up of the situation: he was tactful and complimentary about
Banks's support for the expedition. However, he was more outspoken
regarding his nautical knowledge:

> To many it will no doubt appear strange that Mr Banks should attempt
> to over rule the opinions of the two great Boards who have the sole
> management of the whole Navy of Great Britain and likewise the opin-
> ions of the principal sea officers concern'd in the expedition; for a
> Gentleman of Mr Banks's Fortune and Abilities to engage in these kind
> of Voyages is as uncommon as it is meritorious and the great additions
> he made last Voyage to the Systems of Botany and Natural History
> gain'd him great reputation which was increased by his imbarking in
> this. This, together with a desire in every one to make things as con-
> venient to him as possible, made him to be consulted on every occasion
> and his influence was so great that his opinion was generally followed,
> was it ever so inconsistent, in preference to those who from their long
> experience in Sea affairs might be supposed better judges . . .[1]

It is difficult to believe that James Cook did not know beforehand
that the ship would be unseaworthy. He had been sailing similar ships
for so long, in so many different sailing conditions, that his seaman's
eye would have known the ship to be unstable long before she left the
yard at Deptford. Perhaps he hoped and suspected that this would be
the case, for it would solve his problem at a simple stroke. But if he did
suspect that the ship was top-heavy, he characteristically kept his
mouth shut and did not communicate his thoughts to anybody. In
the early stages of the alterations he seemed to think that Banks's
improvements would not hinder the working of the ship. If this was
the case, then he was just plain lucky to get his own way without
raising a stink with the Admiralty. He was ready enough with his
opinions after the sea trial:

> Mr Banks unfortunate for himself set out upon too large a Plan a Plan
> that was incompatible with a Scheme of discovery at the Antipodes; had
> he confined himself to the same plan as he set out upon last Voyage,
> attended only to his own persutes and not interfered with the choice,

equipmint and even Direction of the Ships things that he was not a competent judge of, he would have found every one concerned in the expedition ever ready to oblige him, for my self I can declare it: instead of finding fault with the Ship he ought to have considered that the *Endeavour* Bark was just such another . . .²

Cook proposed to cut down the poop, to shorten the masts and to change the guns from six-to four-pounders. The Navy Board proposed not only to cut down her poop, but to remove the spare deck, lower her waist and to bring her as near as possible back to her original state. She was ordered to put into Sheerness, where on 18 May the officers of that yard received orders to carry out the restoration work.

Poor Joseph Banks was put into a terrible dilemma. His defence was to claim that the wrong ship had been chosen in the first place and that the *Resolution* was totally unfit for the service. He proposed that a forty-gun frigate or an East Indiaman be purchased in her stead: this would give him the space and comfort he so much wanted. James Cook would have none of it. He considered both of these proposed vessels 'to have been highly improper for making discoveries in remot[e] parts . . .' The clamour became so great that for a time it looked as though the issue would come before the House of Commons, but the Admiralty and the Navy Board got their act together and began to demolish the superfluous decks. Banks and Solander arrived at Sheerness soon afterwards and, according to John Elliott's account, Banks 'swore and stamped upon the Wharfe, like a Mad Man, and instantly ordered his Servants and all his things out of the Ship'. Joseph declared that if the *Resolution* were to be returned to its original condition, then he was not prepared to go on the voyage. He seemed to expect that his threat to withdraw from the expedition would bring the Admiralty to their senses and that he would get his East Indiaman. The Admiralty took no notice. Banks returned to London in a huff, and the news soon followed that he and his party had withdrawn their support for the expedition. They beat a hasty retreat and planned instead to make a journey to Iceland to study the flora and fauna in the northern as opposed to the southern latitudes.

The problem of choosing the leader for the expedition had therefore solved itself. But another botanist, or two botanists, had to be found to replace Banks and Solander. Provisioning the ships and mustering the crews went ahead as the day of departure came nearer and other problems surfaced. The bread that had been loaded on to both ships was mouldy even before the ships had left port. This problem was quickly solved when it was discovered that the mould had been caused by lining the bread rooms with unseasoned timber. Cook himself was not beyond criticism. Robert Cooper complained that the captain had not told anybody about the stowage arrangement for the ship and this lack of data was preventing the first lieutenant from making decisions about berths and storage. Cook was probably still pondering the most efficient way of storing everything aboard the ship, but one of his faults was that it was against his nature to discuss decisions such as these democratically with his officers. At the end of May, Hugh Palliser, the comptroller of the Navy and a great supporter of James Cook, arrived to inspect the ship. On 10 June, Palliser's visit was followed by that of the First Lord of the Admiralty, the Earl of Sandwich.

On Sunday morning, 21 June, James Cook took leave of his family; this was an emotional scene for which he supplies no details. He set out for Sheerness accompanied by the official astronomer, William Wales. The ship was almost ready to sail for Plymouth, but she had to wait until 25 June for a fair wind. Clerke recorded the departure from Sheerness in his journal:

> ... at 2 cast off the Bridles & sail'd out of the Harbour to the Nore with several of the Officers of the Yard on board. A fine fresh Breeze – haul'd upon a wind on purpose to try what effect these alterations had made upon our Ship and soon found to our very great satisfaction that it had entirely remedied every ill quality she had – found her now a stiff Ship – work'd well – and readily got very good way through the Water.[3]

The *Resolution* continued to handle well on the voyage through the English Channel and along the south coast. She was a smart-looking ship, with a prancing horse as a figure-head, and she had a complement of 112 men of whom a few require a brief introduction. We have already met Cook's first lieutenant, Robert Palliser Cooper, an unemotional man but a steady and reliable officer. His middle name was chosen because of his relationship to Sir Hugh Palliser, the comptroller of the Navy to whom Cook owed so much for the development of his own naval career. The second lieutenant was Charles Clerke, the man who was so critical of Banks's 'improvements' to the ship. He had sailed as third lieutenant with Cook on the *Endeavour* and the captain therefore knew him to be a reliable officer. The third lieutenant, Richard Pickersgill, was born in West Tanfield. He had also sailed round the world on the *Endeavour* voyage, and prior to that with Samuel Wallis on the *Dolphin* – at the age of only twenty-three, Pickersgill was starting off on his third circumnavigation of the world! He liked the grog, but he was a good officer and navigator, and Cook knew from his previous voyage that he was capable of finding a longitude by the method of lunars.

There were several others on the *Resolution* who had been shipmates on the *Endeavour*. They included the gunner Robert Anderson from Inverness and his fellow Scotsman James Gray of Leith. There was Isaac Smith, Cook's young relative by marriage, who had been the first to set foot on the east coast of Australia at the age of fourteen – he was now eighteen and a useful surveyor and draughtsman. Solomon Reading the boatswain's mate, the Irishman John Marra, midshipman William Harvey, William Collett from High Wycombe, William Peckover the gunner's mate and the ship's carpenter Edward Terrell had all sailed on the *Endeavour* and had signed up to sail again with Cook. When the contingent of marines joined the ship at Sheerness, they included two *Endeavour* men – Lieutenant John Edgecumbe and Corporal Samuel Gibson. The latter had run off with a local girl in Tahiti and had been punished by Cook for his desertion, but he bore no malice towards the captain.

The ship's surgeon was James Patten, a steady and very professional man. The surgeon's mate was William Anderson, a self-taught naturalist skilled at preparing botanical and zoological specimens and also an excellent linguist. The ship's master, Joseph Gilbert, was from Boston in Lincolnshire and had served on the *Guernsey* during the survey of Newfoundland and Labrador. The sail-maker Richard Rollett was from Lynn in Norfolk; he kept a journal scribbled between the pages of his Bible. Richard Grindall, an able seaman aged twenty-two, is worthy of mention. He was one of the few men who sailed with Cook and also fought at Trafalgar. He rose through the ranks to command the *Prince* at the Battle of Trafalgar and he was promoted to vice-admiral at the end of his long career. The youngest of the midshipmen were John Elliott, a native of the Yorkshire market town of Helmsley, aged fifteen; Alexander Hood, aged only fourteen, who had excellent naval connections and was a nephew of the Admiral Lord Hood; and another youngster, about the same age as Elliott, a quiet and inoffensive young man who made hardly made any impression on the voyage but who was destined to have a great Canadian city named after him. His name was George Vancouver. These three formed a firm friendship with each other, and their exploits surfaced occasionally during the voyage, particularly those of John Elliott, who wrote a good account of the voyage much later in life. Cook sent them aloft with the sailors to learn the ropes.

There was much rejoicing at the Burney household in Queen Square when young James Burney was given his opportunity to sail with Cook. James was not an officer: he signed on as an able-bodied seaman and when Captain Cook saw Burney he must have remembered his own first day in the Royal Navy, when he, too, had signed on with the same lowly rank. Burney was a talented and well-educated man and a great asset to the voyage. He was very sociable and he enjoyed playing cards. He quickly made a good impression on Cook. This was just as well, for Charles Burney had extracted a gentleman's agreement from Lord Sandwich that his son should be promoted as soon as the opportunity arose. William Wales came as the official astronomer: his home was near Wakefield in Yorkshire and he was married to the sister of Charles Green, the astronomer on Cook's first voyage. Wales was a good-humoured man who entertained his shipmates with anecdotes delivered in his colourful north-country accent. In later life he was said to resemble Mr Pickwick. He was accompanied by his servant, George Gilpin. William Hodges joined the ship a few days after her arrival at Plymouth. He was the official artist of the voyage and was destined to do a great deal towards recording the events of the voyage for posterity.

A botanist called Francis Masson also joined the ship at Plymouth. His job was to collect specimens for the Royal Botanical Gardens at Kew, but he did not intend to sail around the world: he planned to leave the ship and return to England from Cape Town. The ship's official naturalists were Johann Reinhold Forster, who at forty-three was only a year younger than Cook, and his eighteen-year-old son George Forster. When the Forsters heard that the Banks party had

walked out on the voyage, they quickly volunteered to come as replace-
ments; they joined the ship at Sheerness with all the baggage and
paraphernalia of two avid collectors of flora and fauna. It is natural to
assume that it was the father who had generated the son's interest in
botany and zoology but in fact, as Forster's autobiography explains, it
was the son who first inspired the father:

> When he [George aged four or five] saw the insects and new plants
> coming out in the garden with the first signs of spring, he wanted to
> know in detail the name of each insect, each flower, each bird. Although
> I had learned in Berlin and Halle in company with a friend of my youth,
> Dr Jampert, some natural history from the writings of the great Linné
> [Linnaeus], this certainly did not suffice enough on the one hand to give
> instruction and, on the other, it had long been forgotten again. I wanted
> to satisfy the inquisitiveness of my dear son; accordingly, soon after-
> wards, I went on foot into Danzig and purchased the Halle edition
> of Linné's *Systema Naturae*, together with Ludwig's *Definitiones Generum
> plantarum*, edited by Boehmer, and the *Philosophica botanica* of the great
> Linné; I then commenced to learn natural history anew with great
> industry and to make myself acquainted, aided by these and other books
> which my friends passed on to me, with the plants, birds, fishes and
> reptiles of my neighbourhood: then I dictated the names as well as the
> peculiarities, economy and characteristics of the plants and animals to
> my son.[4]

The two Forsters arrived penniless in England in October 1766,
when young George was twelve years old. Johann left his pregnant wife
behind in Danzig with five children to look after. He hoped to make his
fortune in England and to bring his family to join him when he became
established. It is difficult to sympathise with Forster over his poverty
when we find that he had spent a fortune on scientific equipment and
had set up a library of over a thousand books. In England, he managed
to obtain a post at the Warrington Academy, where his duties included
teaching as well as academic research. The Warrington Academy was
an educational institution which existed for just under thirty years,
from 1757 until 1786 and it was the life work of its founder, the Revd
John Seddon (1724–70). In its short life, this establishment achieved a
very high academic status. The academy's most famous teacher was
the scientist Joseph Priestley, who taught genteel literature and classics

but not science. He and Forster may have met each other at Warrington, but Forster was effectively Priestley's replacement and so the two never actually worked together.

Forster resented some of his duties, which included the teaching of a class of unruly fourteen year olds, but in five years at Warrington he produced a large number of published papers which served to enhance the reputation of the academy. He was soon corresponding with Banks and Solander and with other members of the Royal Society in London. The journey from Lancashire to London seemed no obstacle to him and we find him visiting Joseph Banks in New Burlington Street. Soon, he was able to bring his wife Justina and six children over from Danzig to live with him at the Warrington Academy. In 1768 he was dining with Anna Blackburne at Orford Hall near Warrington and arranging and classifying her insect collection – soon afterwards, he was exchanging specimens with Pallas and Linnaeus. Judging by a letter written to Forster, Linnaeus thought very highly of him. When he found that the Forsters had replaced Joseph Banks on the voyage with James Cook, Linnaeus wrote to Forster full of praise for the expedition's new botanist:

> He [Cook] could not have chosen a more outstanding man. The very fact that you, a man of mature years, have dared to leave behind your wife and family and, with your famous son, to undertake so perilous a journey, spurred by the love of knowledge, shows a spirit of heroism which rivals that of the heroes of war.[5]

The Forsters were promised a fee of £4,000 for their part in the expedition. Justina Forster's children were to lose their father again, but at least they were provided for financially. Johann Forster had his faults, but he was a very acute observer: his journal is well written, full of detailed observations of humanity as well as scientific details, and this alone was a great asset to the voyage. He brought with him a servant called Ernest Scholient who contributed very little to the enterprise. If the letter from Linnaeus is representative, then young George Forster had already made a name for himself. The drawings of the botanical specimens that he produced are proof of superb draughtsmanship: he could bring out in three-dimensional reality all the main features of his specimens – the thorns, berries, leaves and flowers drawn with subtle shadings of light.

The *Adventure* was a smaller ship than the *Resolution*, with a complement of only eighty-one; she was strongly built, bluff in the bows, with a nymph for her figure-head. Her captain was Tobias Furneaux, aged thirty-seven. He was from a Devonshire family and, like Pickersgill, had already sailed around the world with Samuel Wallis, who happened to be his cousin by marriage. Cook found Furneaux a pleasant and agreeable man; he was an excellent choice for the job. As the voyage progressed, the occasional difference surfaced between the two captains, but this was because Furneaux was unable to live up to the perfectionist standards required by Cook.

The *Adventure*'s first lieutenant was Joseph Shank, who unfortunately suffered from gout and consequently was unable to complete the voyage – he returned home from Cape Town. Arthur Kempe was the second lieutenant. In 1758 he had served in Quebec and he probably knew Cook from his time in Canada. The ship's master was Peter Fannin, who was probably a Manxman and certainly retired to the Isle of Man after the voyage was over, to set up a school of navigation. John Wilby must be mentioned: he was only an able-bodied seaman but he kept a valuable journal of the voyage and gained promotion when he returned to England. The quartermaster was William Sowrey from Lancaster and his colleague William Facey was from the same town. The marines numbered thirteen, with John Mullineux as sergeant and Alexander Mills as corporal.

The *Adventure* mustered only four supernumeraries, two of whom were secretaries to Joseph Banks and therefore left the ship before she sailed. The other two were the astronomer William Bayly and his servant Robert Macky. Bayly was a farmer's son born at Bishop's Cannings in Wiltshire. He had served in the household of the third Duke of Richmond at his Goodwood estate and he had also been an assistant at the Royal Greenwich Observatory. As was customary, the ships' decks bore some resemblance to a farmyard, being well stocked with sheep, cows, pigs, hens, ship's cats and dogs, not to mention a multitude of rats. It might be worth mentioning the number of sailors who deserted: fifty-eight from the *Resolution* and thirty-seven from the *Adventure*. It is true that Cook had gained a good reputation as a humane captain and that many of his crew had volunteered to sail with him again. It is also true that the common sailor's image of a long voyage was one of hardship, scurvy and dying seamen. There were a great many sailors who recoiled in horror at the thought of a three-year journey around the world, the greater part of the voyage spent at sea in cramped conditions, with stale water and nothing to eat except the atrocious ship's food of salted meat and biscuits flavoured with weevils. Naval discipline was maintained by fear: offences were punished by tying the offenders to a grating and lashing them with the cat-o'-nine-tails. Cook was very humane by the standards of the day but even he occasionally resorted to the lash when he felt it was necessary: otherwise there was a danger that the men might conclude he was a soft touch. The common sailor had little or no rights once he had made his mark to agree to the voyage. If the ship's complement was short, the traditional method of recruitment was for the press gang to make a tour of the dockside taverns to help muster the crew; the bullying tactics of the gang were perfectly legal when manning the Royal Navy.

The two astronomers were well equipped with telescopes and navigational equipment. They also carried responsibility for the ship's chronometers. The art of navigation had taken a great step forward in the previous few years and no unbiased person could doubt that Harrison's fourth marine chronometer had proved a remarkable success. In 1765 he had been granted half the Board of Longitude prize of £20,000 for building a successful timepiece for keeping time at sea – the other £10,000 was a few more years in coming. By 1772 Harrison's chronometer had been successfully copied by Larcum Kendall of Furnival's Inn Court and it was Kendall's copy that was to be taken on the voyage. John Arnold of the Adelphi had also made three chronometers based on his own design principles; these machines were not as well tested as Kendall's but they, too, were made available for the voyage. One went to the *Resolution* with the Kendall chronometer, the other two went to the *Adventure*.

The ships carried two pieces of apparatus for making fresh water from sea water. One was the Irving apparatus that consisted of a large copper vessel to heat the water on the cook's fire – a heat source which seldom went out during the voyage. The steam from the boiling sea water was distilled to give pure water. The second method used an experimental apparatus called Osbridge's machine, which consisted of several sheets of plated sheet iron trays with holes like a colander. The water was pumped from the bottom tray to the top and allowed to filter down through the trays to the bottom. The machine had to be set to the side of the ship for the breeze to take away the stench. Cook claimed it was 'an excellent contrivance for sweetening water at sea', but after giving it a fair trial he found it consumed a lot of fuel. The age-old method of collecting rainwater in a sail was also used, but this was of limited value in the tropics where the rainfall was very unpredictable. The rations included eighty barrels of sauerkraut, amounting to two pounds per man per week for three years. This was the main anti-scorbutic diet, but other anti-scorbutic measures included a sweet wort made from malt. The ships also carried orange and lemon preservatives but these were not held in bulk and were only given to sufferers of scurvy at the discretion of the ship's surgeon.

Cook's status as an explorer was held in such high esteem by the Admiralty that he had effectively been able to write his own sailing plans for the voyage. It seemed reasonable to sail the higher latitudes in the southern hemisphere, searching for new land. The first part of the plan was therefore to sail for New Zealand via the Cape of Good Hope and to explore the southern latitudes of the Indian Ocean on this first leg of the journey. The ships were to keep together, but if they became separated they would make for a rendezvous at Queen Charlotte Sound between the North and South Islands of New Zealand. It was known from the previous voyage that the ships could be watered and re-provisioned at Queen Charlotte Sound.

Upon due consideration of the discoveries that have been made in the Southern Ocean and the tracks of the Ships which have made these discoveries; it appears that no Southern lands of great extent can extend to the Northward of 40° of Latitude, except about the Meridian of 140° West, every other part of the Southern Ocean have at different times been explored to the northward of the above parallel. Therefore to make new discoveries the Navigator must Traverse or Circumnavigate the Globe in a higher parallel than has hitherto been done, and this will be best accomplished by an Easterly Course on account of the prevailing westerly winds in all high Latitudes. The principal thing to be attended to is the proper Seasons of Year, for Winter is by no means favourable for discoveries in these Latitudes; for which reason it is humbly proposed that the Ships may not leave the Cape of Good Hope before the latter

end of September or beginning of October, when having the whole
summer before them may safely Steer to the Southward and make their
way to New Zealand, between the parallels of 45° and 60° or in as high
a Latitude as the weather and other circumstances will admit. If no land
is discovered in this rout the Ships will be obliged to touch at New
Zealand to recrute their water.[6]

What happened after reaching New Zealand depended on what discoveries had been made, but the general plan was to winter in Tahiti
and to return via Cape Horn:

From New Zealand the same rout must be continued to Cape Horn, but
before this can be accomplished they will be overtaken by Winter, and
must seek Shelter in the more Hospitable Latitudes, for which purpose
Qtahieta will probably be found to be the most convenient, at, and in
its Neighbourhood the Winter Months may be spent, after which they
must steer to the Southward and continue their rout for Cape Horn in
the Neighbourhood of which they may again recrute their water, and
afterwards proceed for the Cape of Good Hope.[7]

Cook sketched the proposed route for Lord Sandwich to see on a
map of the world:

The yellow line on the Map shews the track I would propose the Ships
to make, Supposeing no land to intervene, for if land is discovered the
track will be altered according to the directing of the land, but the
general rout must be pursued otherwise some part of the Southern
Ocean will remain unexplored.[8]

The surprising thing about Cook's route is that he had no plans for
the further exploration of the coast of Australia. From Cook's charting
of the east coast, combined with the Dutch discoveries on the west, it
seemed obvious that Australia was one large island – it was the only
landmass in the southern seas to approach the size of the fabled *Terra
Australis Incognita*. There was a huge uncharted gap in the Australian
coastline, however, on the Great Australian Bight, and there were
smaller gaps to the north. It was still possible, though highly improb-
able, that New Holland and New South Wales were separate islands.
There was also a question mark around Van Dieman's Land, the land
discovered by Tasman in 1642. This discovery was assumed by the

geographers to belong to the same landmass as New South Wales, a theory that was entirely wrong, but the *Endeavour* had not managed to chart the coastline between her own landfall in Australia and that of Tasman in Van Dieman's Land (Tasmania). James Cook, having sighted the south-east coast of Australia, decided to follow the coast to the west and the north. It seems entirely out of character that he was not curious to know what lay to the south and the east of his landfall. The same argument can be applied to the far north of Australia. It was understandable, essential in fact, that the *Endeavour* made straight for the nearest civilization after passing Cape York. However, there was still coast to be charted to the west of Cape York and Cook seemed to have no more inclination to explore this coastline than to explore the southern end of his Australian discoveries.

Certainly, the charting of the east coast of Australia had been dangerous and almost suicidal. The *Endeavour* very nearly perished when she struck on the Great Barrier Reef and was unable to move for a whole day. Two months later, she came even closer to disaster when she was caught in a flat calm with a strong tide carrying her at speed towards certain death on the reef. Cook knew that the second ship would be of little use in the flat calm, but with two vessels the crew and provisions could be saved if there was a repetition of the first of these disasters. Perhaps it was the dangerous nature of the Australian coast that caused Cook to ignore it on his second voyage. The coast was destined to claim many more victims than the *Endeavour* as more ships came to explore the area, but a danger known is a danger lessened and it still seems out of character for Cook not to have returned to Australia. We can only conclude that the appeal of new discoveries in the higher latitudes meant more to him and more to the British Admiralty.

The Pacific Ocean, covering more than a quarter of the Earth's surface, still had great expanses of water where no ship had ever sailed. Over a period of two and a half centuries, many isolated sightings had been made in the Pacific. All of these were small islands, nearly all were mere sightings and not landings, and many lay unvisited since their first discovery. The positions of these islands were very uncertain. In 1521, Magellan's ships sighted two uninhabited islands as they crossed the Pacific. These are now thought to have been Puka Puka and Caroline

Atoll – but the only clue to their location was the date of the sightings from his log. In 1579, the Englishman Francis Drake saw only one island, Tidore, before he reached Java, but he crossed the Pacific from the Bay of San Francisco and his crossing was almost entirely north of the Equator. In the same century, the Spaniard Mendana made two forays into the Pacific: on his first voyage (1568), he discovered the Solomon Islands and on his second voyage many years later (1595), he discovered a group of islands which he named the Marquesas after his patron the Marques of Canete. In the following century, the passion for exploration had abated and the most notable voyage as regards the Pacific Ocean was that of Tasman in 1642–3. Tasman did not actually cross the Pacific: he circumnavigated Australia from his base at Batavia but without seeing anything of the Australian coastline. His voyage of little over a year was very short compared to those of other navigators, but for well over a century his ship was the only one to have landed at Tasmania and New Zealand, and he also discovered the Tonga and Fiji island groups.

There were plenty of people who still believed that there could be a continent in the southern Pacific. One of these was Alexander Dalrymple, who had been one of the main protagonists for the *Endeavour* voyage. Dalrymple may have been discredited over his ideas for the great southern continent, but he was no fool and he had not been idle in the preceeding few years. He had published his book *Collection of Voyages and Discoveries in the South Pacific Ocean*. It was a very valuable work, covering exactly what the title implied, details of all the known voyages into the Pacific Ocean with the discoveries made over two and a half centuries. Some of the accounts were very reliable, but the navigators of old had no way of determining a precise longitude for the islands. The Pacific Ocean was still a source of traveller's tales and sailor's yarns, of dusky maidens, mythical people, sea monsters and strange creatures. It was so many generations since the islands in Dalrymple's book had been sighted that they had become mythical places of folklore. Cook wanted to change them from myth into fact. He wanted to rediscover them, to calculate their correct longitude, to tidy up the map of the Pacific, to put them in their correct positions and to chart them for future navigators. This was the second great objective of the voyage. It was a formidable task and impossible to achieve in a single voyage, but he intended to visit as many islands as possible in the time available to him.

The officers, crew and supernumeraries had all arrived in Plymouth. Johann Forster started to keep his journal before he left England. One of his early entries is an uncomplimentary impression of eighteenth-century Plymouth, with details of the sewage disposal arrangements:

> Plymouth is a place with narrow irregular winding streets, which have a Channel running fresh water in their middle, & though this is a great inconvenience to carriages, which must always have one wheel in the channel, & to people walking in the Streets, who are constantly splashed by the horses; it has in the other hand the Advantage of carrying off all the filth & impurities of the town, especially at night, when the contents of a great many pots with humane excrements are emptied into it, as few people have regular little houses in this town. The recession of the Sea at ebbtide leaves a great part of the interior harbour dry & causes an intolerable stench.[9]

On 12 July 1772, the lieutenants and the astronomers landed on Drake Island to set the chronometers and wind them in preparation for the voyage ahead. All four had kept good time to date and at last the ships were ready for their voyage to the ends of the earth. There was a fair breeze early the following day, and at six in the morning, as the sun was driving the sea mist from Plymouth Sound, the *Resolution* and the *Adventure* weighed anchor and set their sails for the open sea. 'Farewell Old England,' wrote Richard Pickersgill with a great flourish in his journal. Would he be lucky enough to return to England for a third time?

> A wet sheet and a flowing sea,
> A wind that follows fast,
> And fills the white and rustling sail
> And bends the gallant mast —
> And bends the gallant mast, my boys,
> While, like the eagle free,
> Away the good ship flies, and leaves
> Old England on the lee.[10]
>
> Allan Cunningham (1784–1842)

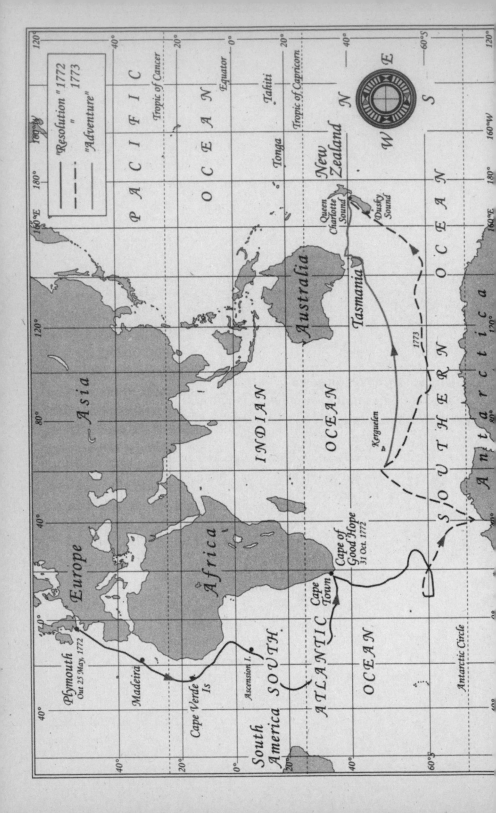

THREE

Cape Town and Antarctica

All together they veered out the sheet, and in unison they let out the sails now to port, then to starboard: together they turned and turned again the yards high above: the wind they wanted carried the fleet along.

Aeneid, v, 830

In spite of the major reconstructions that had given her framework a hammering, the *Resolution* sailed well and even better than Cook had expected. The steering was positive, she was a good stiff ship and he could set the topsails even in a gale-force wind. The problem was the *Adventure*: she was too unstable to set her topsails in a high wind, so the *Resolution* frequently had to stop and wait for her consort. In normal sailing conditions, they were well matched and there was little to choose between the two sloops. When they were together, they would sometimes race against each other and the *Resolution* usually proved the faster ship. This was not always the case, however, for the *Adventure* could turn more rapidly than her sister and in certain weather conditions the larger ship found herself outsailed by the smaller. Clerke noted one such occurrence in his journal:

The *Adventure* run ahead of us which I think as times go is a very remarkable occurrence and was oblig'd to shorten'd a good deal of sail and back her Mizen Tops[ails] to get astern again. She is sharper about the Bows than the *Resolution* and in a heavy Head Sea she will sometimes wrong us a little, this is the second time we observ'd it during the 10 weeks we've been out – every other of the 68 days out of the 70 our distance had been somewhat curtail'd and many of them considerably by staying for Her.[1]

On 23 July, when the ships were off the coast of Portugal, three large vessels were sighted. One of them flew the English colours from her stern, but as the British approached the flags were taken down and replaced with the Spanish colours. The ships were Spanish men-of-war and the leading vessel fired a shot across the bows of the *Adventure*, forcing her to heave to. It was just as well that the English ships were not named the *Raleigh* and the *Drake*, for the three Spanish warships mustered nearly two hundred guns between them and, had they felt so inclined, could have blown the new expedition to smithereens with one double broadside. The Spanish asked Captain Furneaux the name of the ship ahead and he replied that it was Captain Cook's ship, the *Resolution*. The Spanish knew all about Cook's discoveries in the south seas. They respected the explorer and intended no malice. They allowed the ships to sail on and wished them a *bon voyage*.

At the end of the month, the small convoy arrived at the island of Madeira, where they were able to stock up on fresh meat and vegetables, as well as the excellent wine. Cook passed on some gossip he had picked up from the British Consul. It seemed that Joseph Banks had arranged for another member of his party to join the ship at Madeira. The person was a botanist who went by the name of Mr Burnett and who, for a reason soon to be disclosed, had been unable to join the ship in England. The botanist was aged about thirty and was described as 'rather ordinary than otherwise', but what followed next showed that Burnett was far from ordinary. The disclosure must have raised a few eyebrows at the Admiralty. It seemed that Joseph Banks had gone to some lengths to ensure his voyage of discovery would be as pleasant as possible.

> Every part of Mr Burnett's behaviour and every action tended to prove that he was a Woman, I have not met with a person that entertains a doubt of a contrary nature, he brought letters of recommendation to an English House where he was accommodated during his stay. It must be observed that Mrs Burnett must have left London about the time we were first ready to sail.[2]

Ms Burnett had already left the island when Cook arrived, but the gossip travelled quickly around the ship and it made some impression on John Elliott, who was only fifteen at the time. Many years later, he mentioned the incident in his memoirs, stating that it 'surprised and amused Captain Cook very much'. His version adds a few interesting details to Cook's account:

> When Capt. Cook waited upon the British Consul, he took the two Forsters, Myself, and another young officer to breakfast with him, who, during our visit, told us that he had been greatly surprised and amused a little time back in consequence of a Gentleman arriving in an American Ship, recommended to him by a Letter from Mr Banks, until the *Resolution* should arrive. That some time after his arrival, the Maid servant by some accident discovered that the said gentleman was a *Lady*. The Maid was greatly astonished, and informed their Master, who, equally surprized as herself, charged her to keep the matter secret, not intending himself to take the least notice of the circumstance to the Lady, until Mr Banks' arrival. But as soon as ever Mr Banks found himself under necessity of giving up his plan of going out in the *Resolution*, he wrote to the Lady to quit Madeira immediately and she had been gone only a week when we arrived.[3]

The next stop was at Porto Praya in the Cape Verde Islands, where fresh water and more supplies were obtained. This afforded the botanists a second opportunity to collect specimens and for George Forster to practise his drawing skills. The Forsters were delighted every time they made landfall and they spent all their available time botanising and enthusing about the flora and fauna of Madeira and the Cape Verde Islands. The naturalists had plenty to do and observe even when the ship was at sea. They took note of all the birds and sea animals that they encountered. One day, there was a heavy shower of rain and a swallow which had been flying about the ship became so wet that it was unable to fly. George Forster carefully nursed and dried the swallow, then set it free to fly around the lower deck. It immediately gorged itself upon the numerous flies. During dinner, it passed through an open porthole and regained its freedom but at about six in the evening it flew back inside. It flew out again and roosted somewhere on the rigging during the night. Early next morning, the swallow came back into the cabin and through to the steerage, where it took its breakfast of flies. It decided to join William Wales the astronomer in his cabin, then it left and was never seen again.

The *Resolution* carried on board some casks of beer brewed with essence of malt. The beer was fermenting and the casks were obviously under great pressure and bursting at the seams, so the barrels were brought on deck and the bungs were removed. There was an explosion like that of a small fowling piece and, to the dismay of the sailors, the precious beer ran out all over the deck. Their dismay was offset by the delight of the ship's goats, which started licking greedily at the deck and were soon staggering around in a drunken stupor. The problem seemed to be that the casks had been warmed by the heat of the tropical sun – had they been stored lower down in the hold where it was cooler, they would have fermented more slowly. There was, however, plenty more alcoholic drink on board and the crew had ample opportunity to show off their drinking prowess when the ship crossed the Equator on 8 September. About fifty of the ship's complement, almost half, underwent the traditional ducking ceremony on their first Crossing of the Line. Others chose to pay for a bottle of brandy to escape the ordeal, and when the liquor began to flow there was much hilarity on board ship. In the evening Forster recorded songs, play and mirth, but we are not given the details of the songs. The weather was calm and Cook therefore knew that there was little danger in having a drunken crew for the day. Furneaux, by contrast, felt that the hilarities would endanger his ship and no such ceremony took place aboard the *Adventure*.

The ships continued their journey south, but they stood out well to the west so that they could make full use of the prevailing winds on the approach to Table Bay. Early in October, the convoy changed course to the east and on the sixteenth of that month they crossed another zero line, that of the Greenwich meridian. They continued on an easterly course and before long land birds were sighted. As they approached closer to the Cape of Good Hope, a greater number of birds appeared near the ships. There were flocks of terns and petrels, and a species of pigeon which they called 'pintadas'. Land was sighted on 30 October and Cook's ship put on all sail to try to enter Table Bay before nightfall. The *Resolution* might have made it, but her escort lay two leagues astern and Cook therefore decided to wait and stand off for the night so that the ships could enter Table Bay together. There was a compensation for the extra day. The sea was full of a small luminous organism identified as

Noctiluca, which glowed strongly phosphorescent during the night. The luminosity was so bright that it appeared as if the whole sea was on fire:

> Scarcely had night spread its darkness on the Surface of the Ocean, when it got the Appearance of being all over a fire. Every wave that broke had a marge of light, perfectly similar to that of a phosphorus, all along the sides of the Ship, where it came in contact with the Sea it seemed to be lined with a stroke of phosphorus. This afforded one of the most agreable & grandest illuminations that ever were beheld. We had a bucket full of this water drawn for Examination & found that in it an infinite number of little round bodies were moving with amazing quickness. When the water was standing during a good time, the sparkling little Objects decreased in number, but by stirring the water, we observed the whole all over luminous: & after leaving it again, the little sparkles moved in different directions very briskly. Though the water with the bucket was suspended the sparkles still kept on moving to & fro', so that it was plain they had a voluntary motion, quite independent of the agitation of the Water or Ship: but however any foreign body coming in contact with the water, caused a new sparkling. Often by stirring in the water, one of these phosphorescent sparks would stick to the hand or finger: we found by a common magnifier, these little atoms were globular, transparent or gelatinous bodies, somewhat brownish.[4]

It was raining the next day as they entered Table Bay, which lay to the north of the town. On one side was Penguin Island and on the other a green promontory. Table Mountain rose majestically behind the town, with the Lion's Rump to the south. To the east was a fort with two batteries and beyond lay the Salt River where other batteries were strategically placed to defend the town. Storehouses and magazines lined the waterfront. The private houses were visible beyond, built in regular spacious streets on rising ground, which gave the residents a fine vista out to sea.

James Cook had been meticulous about health and safety during the passage to Cape Town. He made sure the crew ate their ration of sauerkraut as a precaution against scurvy. He also made sure that the bedding was aired and he fumigated the ship in the tropics when the humid atmosphere caused mould to form on many parts of the ship. At

Porto Praya, where the ship had watered, the sailors took to the local monkeys and sailed with at least fifteen of them on board. The monkeys were a great and popular diversion, but unfortunately they were very dirty and carried disease. Some were 'almost devoured' by lice and Cook had no option but to order them overboard in the interests of hygiene. The losses were not confined to animals. A carpenter, Henry Smock, was lost overboard from the *Resolution* soon after the ship left Porto Praya, and a few days later a man fell overboard from the *Adventure* and, greatly to the consternation of the crew, was taken by a shark. Two midshipmen died from a fever which Furneaux claimed they caught when they were bathing in the tropical heat. Furneaux could have argued that his casualties were a great deal fewer than might have been expected on a voyage of comparable length, and when two outward-bound Dutch East Indiamen arrived at the Cape with heavy losses after a four-month voyage, they seemed to prove the point. One of the Dutch ships had buried 150 men at sea, most of them dead from scurvy, and another sixty were sent straight to the hospital on their arrival at Cape Town.

Joseph Shank, the first lieutenant of the *Adventure*, was a sick man – he had been suffering from gout since the departure from England. Cook made the sensible decision to send him back home. He promoted Arthur Kempe to first lieutenant and took the opportunity to give young James Burney the chance he had been waiting for. Burney was to change ships and become the second lieutenant of the *Adventure*. It took over four months for the news to get back to the house in Queen Square, but on 2 May Fanny Burney put an entry in her diary:

We have had, from the Cape of Good Hope, the Welcome news of my Brother's promotion. Lieutenant Shanks, a young man who was on board the *Adventure*, one of the three sloops under Captain Cook, was so ill, that he was obliged to leave the ship, & return to England, 'in whose place, says the Captain's letter to Lord Sandwich, I have appointed Mr Burney, whom I have found very deserving.' This is most comfortable intelligence – & rejoices us unspeakably; he will be a Lieutenant of 3 years standing by his return. He has written to us, in very good spirits, & assures us that the Cape of Good Hope is a very agreeable place!⁵

Cape Town offered the last opportunity for the explorers to write home. It would be at least another two years before any other messages could be sent. Cook wrote to Joseph Banks, wishing him well and carefully avoiding any references to the gossip from Madeira. He also wrote to John Walker in Whitby. He probably wrote home to his wife, but if so, it was a private letter and we do not know the contents. The botanist Francis Masson remained at Cape Town as arranged, but Johann Forster met another botanist at the Cape, a Swede called Anders Sparrman who had been a pupil of the great Linnaeus himself. Forster must have been impressed with the young man as he persuaded Cook to allow him to join the expedition. The *Resolution* was bursting at the seams with seamen and supernumeraries, but, unlike Johann Rienhold Forster, Sparrman was not a difficult man and Cook agreed to take on the extra body.

One of the Arnold chronometers was accidentally damaged when landing at the Cape. William Wales was seated in the stern of the longboat with the chronometers beside him when the boat was jolted during the landing. Wales did not think it a serious blow, but when they got ashore they discovered that the watch had stopped. The two astronomers, Wales and Baylcy, were soon busy on shore checking the other ship's chronometers. During the voyage, three days before they crossed the Greenwich meridian, there had been an eclipse of the moon. This was an ideal opportunity to calculate the longitude, even though the observation was made in the open sea. The longitude could be calculated by three methods – from the eclipse itself, from the chronometers and by the method of lunars, whereby the moon's position was calculated from the stars. The early part of the eclipse was hidden by cloud, but six measurements were taken of the end of the eclipse. This was the precise time when the last trace of the earth's shadow left the face of the moon. The time was measured by Kendall's chronometer and the eclipse calculation should therefore have given the exact longitude as predicted by the chronometer if the time and the calculations were correct. The six observers were Cook, Forster, Wales, Pickersgill, Gilbert and Harvey, and their timings of the end of the eclipse varied by as much as two minutes. According to Cook, the eclipse gave a figure of $6°33\frac{1}{2}'$ W for the longitude, but according to Forster the figure was $6°46'$. The method of lunars, using the quadrant to measure the distance from the moon's limb to the fixed stars, gave a figure of 6°13'. Using the Kendall chronometer, a simple calculation gave a longitude of 7°9'. The difference between the lunar and chronometer methods was therefore fifty-two nautical miles. The astronomers were in agreement that the figure calculated from the eclipse was likely to be the most accurate of the three. The other two methods were probably within thirty or forty nautical miles of the true position, but the errors show how difficult it was to get an accurate figure for the longitude even with the best instruments available at the time.

Cook was still a little apprehensive about the chronometers. One of the problems with them was that the errors always accumulated and at intervals they had to be checked against the stars and reset to the correct time. He gave measured praise to Kendall's timepiece, however, and as the voyage progressed he began to trust it more and more. One of the three Arnold chronometers was keeping good time, so both ships carried a reliable timepiece.

The first leg of the journey, from England to Cape Town, had been relatively easy, with good watering places, well-stocked islands for provisions and warm tropical seas. The next leg was the passage to New Zealand, but Cook had no intention of taking the straightforward route. His plan was to sail directly south to where the uncharted waters began. It would soon test the mettle of the seamen as the exploration of the far south got under way. It was early summer in the southern hemisphere, but there was a chill in the air soon after they left the Cape of Good Hope. The next day, Cook gave out the issue of warm clothing for all the men, the fearnought jackets and trousers which were supplied by the Admiralty. The contractor had tried to skimp on the material: the sleeves and jackets were too short but the enterprising seamen lengthened them with baize and made matching caps of baize and canvas. Nobody knew when the next fresh water would be found, so water was strictly rationed and it was necessary to use cold sea water for washing. Four days out from the Cape, Johann Forster was already complaining about the damp and the cold. His cabin was next to that of the ship's master, Joseph Gilbert, and the space between was taken up by one of the guns. Cook was prepared to stow the gun in the hold after leaving Cape Town and, according to Forster, the extra space was offered to Joseph Gilbert but he refused it. When Forster tried to claim the space for himself, the ship's master changed his mind:

> The Capt said to me, the room was very little, but that when we would have passed the Cape, he would give me in the room which the Gun abaft my Cabin now takes up: for he could stow it then away. He added he had before offerred this place to the Master for enlarging his Cabbin, but that he refused it, I might therefore have it. When I wished to have the Gun taken into my Cabbin, the Master claimed that space as his, the Capt then told him he had refused it; but he insisted it was his, & though the Captain had promised it to me, he then found himself under necessity to disoblige us both, by declaring none should have it. Were my Cabbin larger I could sling a Cot in it: by which means I would gain more room & more light, & my Cot could be thus disposed, that it could not leak on my head; whereas I must now be exposed to the Injuries of weather by the foolish obstinacy of the Master.[6]

There was a more serious problem in the middle of the night when it was found that the ship was taking in water. A search revealed that a small porthole had been cut in the bosun's store to allow some daylight into a room where candles were too dangerous to use. The porthole was broken and it was very close to the waterline, the water was pouring in and the level was rising steadily, but once the problem had been located it was quickly repaired. The ships were sailing well and making good progress, from sixty to a hundred miles per day, and the temperature fell to below freezing. Soon the first icebergs appeared. They were a novel sight to most of the crew, creating great excitement as the men thought that they had discovered islands. The mountains of ice were drifting north from the Antarctic and were over two hundred feet tall, towering high above the ships, but they left a wake behind them and it was soon obvious that they consisted only of great floating masses of ice. Forster made some calculations to try to ascertain how much of each iceberg was under water.

It was on the icebergs that they saw what appeared to be a sign of land, for some of them were populated by Antarctic penguins. The elder Forster wanted to take a penguin as a specimen. He succeeded, but not without some difficulty. These strange, regimented and uniformed

creatures were a great novelty. Pickersgill thought that they performed
their evolutions so well that they wanted only the use of arms to cut
a figure on parade on Wimbledon Common, and he gave the most
entertaining description of the penguins:

> They are in general about the size of a duck but stand Errect on their
> feet; and from their white breasts are not unjustly likened to children
> with white bibs on by Sir John Narborough [a seventeenth-century
> explorer]. We fired a 4 p[oun]d. ball at them on which they very regularly
> wheeld off in ranks two by two, and in that order march'd down to the
> water.[7]

It was established that the icebergs were made from fresh water
rather than sea water, and that they could therefore solve one of the
ship's major supply problems by providing a virtually infinite quantity
of drinking water. The first attempts to break pieces of ice off the bergs
proved very difficult. It was very dangerous to approach too close to a
melting iceberg. As the sun heated the icebergs, the splitting of the ice
would sometimes give off a great crack as loud and sudden as the firing
of one of the ship's cannons. Unpredictable avalanches of ice and snow
could crash down on the ship at any time. In the wake of the moving
icebergs, however, there was a trail of smaller fragments of ice. If they
were not too large, these fragments could be hoisted out of the water
and on to the ship. William Hodges produced a very fine watercolour
painting showing the taking on of ice by the *Resolution* at a latitude of
61° S. The procedure was still attended by some risk. The smaller
icebergs were sometimes hard to spot and if the ship ran against
them, they created another navigational hazard. The botanist Anders
Sparrman gave his account of the dangers:

> The sight of icebergs and the danger of their proximity became an
> ordinary event, and one that produces little comment. But there was
> one iceberg in particular that deserves remark, which was half a mile in
> circumference and about 400 feet high. With a movement that was
> hardly noticeable in the water, this enormous mass suddenly lost its
> balance, and nearly rolled over, so that its base or bottom, was turned
> up; yet as far as the eye could judge, this did not seem to increase its
> elevation above the level of the water. On another occasion we

approached a mass of ice, one hundred feet high, with a circumference of at least three miles. Driven by the wind, the great resistance of such an enormous ice colossus must necessarily meet with a corresponding displacement of water; the waves, breaking tremendously, rose high above the iceberg with a violent roar, in a fury of foaming froth.

Often we saw and heard huge masses of ice splitting away from the bergs and go hurtling into the sea with a measured crash; undoubtedly this violence and damage produced the varying and often picturesque shapes of the icebergs in the form of caves, chasms, crevices and peaks, which at times provided a change from the otherwise wearisome monotony of sea, ice and horizon.[8]

The icebergs were a hazard to navigation, but they did have their uses. Cook proceeded very cautiously and, except for the watering, kept well clear of them. They were not the only hazard in the Antarctic seas, for soon a thick fog descended, so dense that they could not see from one end of the ship to the other. The fog continued for several days, and when William Wales and Johann Forster went out in one of the boats to measure the water temperature, they lost sight of the ships in the fog. It was a frightening situation to be lost in the Antarctic. They banged and shouted, making as much noise as possible in their attempt to find the ships, but it was two long hours before they were rescued. The *Resolution* and the *Adventure* managed to stay in touch with each other by firing the occasional gun and the marines would beat regularly upon their drums. The fog was the worst possible weather condition for sighting land, but there were plenty of clear days in between. The daily weather conditions consisted invariably of snow and sleet. Pickersgill told of a gale that sprang up from the north-west. 'One of the greatest seas I ever saw,' he wrote. 'The ships laboured very much, as they both was very loaded and heavy, the water constantly washed over them, which with sleet, rain, and constant anxiety for fear of seeing land to the leeward made it a very uneasy situation.'

Christmas Day 1772 came and went: the seamen had their celebration and were suitably drunk for the occasion. The entertainment consisted mainly of boxing matches between the seamen. This was primitive boxing: there was no boxing ring, no referee and no gloves. Anders Sparrman had never seen 'British savages' boxing and he gave

a lengthy and valuable description of the sport when it was still in a
very early stage of its evolution:

> Few people in Sweden understand the methods of boxing, which to
> my mind has never been properly described; some explanation of it
> cannot fail to throw light upon an aspect of human behaviour,
> especially concerning the Christianity and the character of the British
> savages (as well as that of some of our sailors). Therefore I think a
> short impression of it here will provide a change from the narrative
> of the disagreeable, stormy, cold, and dangerous voyage I have so far
> been recounting.
>
> Boxing is a fight, a duel with fists, in which the blows are principally
> aimed at the opponent's eyes, chest, and stomach. Boxing on this occa-
> sion was suggested partly to settle previous disputes which were still
> outstanding, and partly to decide those which had occurred that day
> through some insulting word or action.
>
> This fighting or boxing generally takes place *stante pede*, so that the
> combatants face each other in an upright and standing position; but
> sometimes they fight while sitting down, or rather, in a riding
> position, sitting astride a box or chest. Boxing *stante pede* is the most
> usual method, but all the boxing I saw that day took place sitting
> astride a chest, probably because the contestants were too unsteady
> and incapable of standing on their legs by the time I arrived at the
> display from the dinner-table. The boxing performed in this way had
> a flavour of the wrestling of olden times, although it was a more
> serious affair.[9]

Having set the scene, Sparrman goes on to describe the bloody
details of the fight. While some of the sparring matches were to settle
grievances between the men, others were fought merely to show their
prowess at the sport:

> The two fighters took their positions opposite one another, each astride
> his end of an ordinary seaman's chest, which was not too uncomfortable
> for this purpose. It is worth noting that, without exception, the boxers
> are always stripped naked to the waist. Thus you may imagine, in the
> cold of winter, two half naked opponents taking their places astride a
> chest with all propriety and coolness, and immediately exchanging
> punches aimed with such vigour and strength that the spectator's eyes

can scarcely follow the lightning speed of the fight. You may also imagine the thuds of the diverse attacks upon jaws, foreheads, eyes, stomachs and chests, each impact giving its peculiar sound. Soon the nose and mouth of one or both combatants are bleeding, and the blood splashes about and streaks the divine countenances, over which it is further spread by the increasing blows; also, it gradually becomes apparent how the seamen's knuckles, hard as iron, are imprinting bruises and bloody patches on the respective skins.

Neither of them leaves his place on the chest, or gives in before he collapses, completely exhausted, if not absolutely unconscious. At this moment the spectators always take the loser into their care, refresh, raise, and encourage him (if it can be done) to continue the fight; but once he is down, the winner may not give him a single blow. In these tilting matches on chests they keep to their rules, just as they do when fighting on their feet, such as not pulling each other by the hair or gripping each other round the waist; the whole fight consists in the brutal forward punches, mainly aimed at the eyes. From this cause I had already seen during the voyage the Englishmen's so-called 'black-eyes'; this is *regio oculorum*, the eyelid and its immediate neighbourhood becoming quite black or lead-coloured from the congestion of blood after the blows; this colour, while dispersing, gradually changed to disgusting shades of brown, sea-green and yellow, besides which, the swelling and puffiness in these parts sometimes completely deprived the victim of his sight.[10]

On New Year's Day 1773 they were at a latitude of 60°S. The *Resolution* and *Adventure* were already sailing in latitudes where no ship had sailed before, but from Dalrymple's book and from gossip picked up at Cape Town, Cook knew that earlier in the century a French ship had sighted land to the north-west of their current position. It was in these seas, thirty-four years earlier almost to the day, that the Frenchman Lozier Bouvet had sighted a desolate high rocky cape at a latitude of 54°, but the problem was that the longitude for his sighting could not be trusted. The ships were therefore heading to the west; although it was the wrong direction for New Zealand, Cook wanted to confirm the sighting. With their usual optimism, both the French and the English assumed that Bouvet's Cape was part of a large landmass to the south and Cook therefore assumed that by sailing to the south of the sighting he would find landfall. Bouvet gave his cape the curious

name of Cape Circumcision because January happened to be the Feast
of Circumcision. Several days were spent in the vicinity, but the search
for Bouvet's Cape in the icy seas was in vain. They knew that it was
not worth spending more time searching for what may have been no
more than a floating iceberg. Two days later, Cook felt he had gone
far enough in the wrong direction and he turned back again to the
east.

Conditions were atrocious. Ropes and hawsers were hard with frost
and covered in ice. Freezing icicles covered the superstructure of the
ships. Numb and frozen hands worked the stiff, icy sails. There was
nothing but ice, snow and cold sea breaking over the ships, so cold that
it froze the moment it struck the deck. Temperatures were recorded
between 31 and 35° Fahrenheit, sometimes falling below the freezing
point of 32° Fahrenheit. However, the temperatures were recorded
in daytime, probably at noon, and they took no account of the chill
from the hard, icy wind blowing from the undiscovered Antarctic
continent. At night and in the small hours of the morning, the whole
crew shivered and huddled below decks. The cold was horrific. There
was always a fire in the cook's galley, but most of the time this was the
only heating on the ship, and it was many leagues of ocean to New
Zealand.

The sea was covered in floating pack ice, which Cook referred to as
'field ice'. Two of his crew had served in Greenland's waters and they
had some experience with such conditions. They knew of the dangers
of pack ice and told stories of wooden ships trapped in the ice-field and
crushed to death by the pressure of the ice. Cook continued to sail east
along the ice edge at a cold latitude of 60°. After about two weeks of
running down the sixtieth parallel, the density of the pack ice on the
surface of the sea seemed less and Cook decided it would be safe to sail
nearer to the pole. The ships turned southwards at a longitude of about
40° E, sailing ever closer to the South Pole, though nobody on board
believed that they could ever go so far. At this point of the voyage,
they were further south than any ship had ever sailed before them –
yet still there was nothing but pack ice and no sign of any land. The
morning of 18 January 1773 followed a very short Antarctic night. If
they had arrived three weeks earlier, there would have been no night
at all, for it was close to midsummer and this was the first time that

man had ever entered into the Antarctic Circle. The entry in Cook's journal is under 17 January: this is because of the confusing system of shipboard dating whereby the new day is taken to begin at noon. It is a very routine record for what was an historic occasion – a typical entry, apart from the last sentence:

> In the PM had fresh gales and Clowdy weather. At 6 o'clock, being then in the Latitude of 64°56' S I found the Variation by Gregory's Compass to be 26°41' West, at this time the Motion of the Ship was so great that I could not observe with Dr Knight's Compass. In the AM had hazy weather with Snow Showers and saw but one Island of Ice in the course of these 24 hours so that we begin to think that we have got into a clear Sea. At about ¼ past 11 o'clock we cross'd the Antarctic Circle for at Noon were by observation four Miles and a half South of it and are undoubtedly the first and only ship that ever crossed that line.[11]

Cook's pride manages to show through in spite of his matter-of-fact tone. The ships penetrated south to a latitude of 67°15'. This was estimated to be at longitude 39°35' E. It was an incredible achievement for a sailing ship to penetrate so far into the bitter cold of the Antarctic. It is perhaps just as well that Cook did not know that the Antarctic continent lay only about twenty leagues to the south, as this might have motivated him to take an extra risk to reach the land. However, the pack ice was too solid for the ship to travel any further towards the Pole and he wisely chose to turn around and head back north. He noted that there were plenty of sea birds still following the ship in that cold and silent sea:

> We now saw several Flocks of the Brown and White Pintadoes which we have named Antarctic Petrels because they seem to be natives of that Region. The White Petrels also appear in greater numbers than of late and some few Dark Grey Albatrosses, our constant companions the Blue Petrels have not forsaken us but the Common Pintadoes have quite disappeared as well as many other sorts of which are Common in lower Latitudes.

When at Cape Town, Cook had obtained information about another isolated sighting by Tremarec Kerguelen in the previous year. The Frenchman had called his land *La France Australe* and he optimistically claimed that it was part of a more extensive landmass. Kerguelen had quoted a reasonable latitude of $48\frac{1}{2}°$ S, but, as with Bouvet's Cape Circumcision, his longitude of 57 or 58° E was very unreliable. For the next three weeks, the small convoy headed north and east towards the part of the ocean where Kerguelen had made his sighting.

On 8 February, the inevitable happened. The fog was so thick that the ships could not see each other. In this situation, the agreed arrangement was to fire the guns at intervals. Every time the *Resolution* changed tack, she fired a gun to signal the *Adventure* to do the same. On this day, there was no answering boom. The *Resolution* fired another gun and waited for her consort to reply. Some of the sailors thought they could hear the sounds of the guns in the distance, but others thought that the noise might be no more than a cracking iceberg. The *Resolution* shortened sail, turned and scoured the region of sea where the *Adventure* had last been seen. Cook spent two days searching, but when no sign of the ship was spotted, there was little point in wasting any more time. The ships were separated. But the eventuality was one for which they had made contingency plans – they would meet up again in Queen Charlotte Sound, New Zealand. The incident hindered the search for Kerguelen's land and in the event the *Resolution* passed well to the south of the sighting. Had the island been the great landmass implied by the French, then Cook would certainly have rediscovered it, but the longitude was very inaccurate. He was disappointed again. It was not a great loss. The island did exist; it had fresh water but minimal vegetation. In spite of his claims, Kerguelen had been unable to land on his uninhabited island and Cook would have been faced with very similar problems.

The *Adventure* was lost, stores were low, the food was monotonous. Many men were suffering from colds and other ailments. The elder Forster was constantly in a bad mood and he annoyed everybody by his continual grouching. Morale was low and there were many leagues of ocean still to cover. There was an outbreak of petty pilfering on the ship and Cook was forced to deal with it in the traditional way by flogging the culprits. After twelve weeks at sea, the fearnought jackets were very tattered. The sailors looked like a bunch of scarecrows and they were issued with buttons, needles and thread with which to darn and repair their clothing. Captain Cook stuck dutifully to his plan. He turned again to the south: he had ambitions to cross the Antarctic Circle for a second time. He knew that he had the option of sailing north to New Holland and at this point he could have become the first explorer to chart the southern coastline of Australia. He rejected the idea; it was not part of his sailing instructions and in any case he decided it was safer to head for New Zealand, where he had a rendezvous to keep and he knew that he could get supplies for his men and his ship.

The ship had been at sea for over three months. February was overtaken by March and still they sailed the bitterly cold edge of the frigid southern seas. It was too cold to keep the animals out on the deck: some had already died and the remainder would die if they were not taken below. Cook brought two ewes and a ram below decks, but the elder Forster was not very pleased with the arrangements and most people would sympathise with his dilemma:

We have been obliged to prepare a better & warmer berth for two Ewes & a Ram, which we wished to bring safe to New Zeeland, no more convenient place could be devised than the space between my & the Masters Cabin. I was now beset with cattle & stench on both Sides, having no other but a thin deal partition full of chinks between me & them. The room offered me by Capt Cook, & which the Masters obstinacy deprived me of, was now given to very peaceably bleating creatures, who on a stage raised up as high as my bed, shit & pissed on one side, whilst 5 Goats did the same afore on the other side. My poor Cabin was often penetrated by the wet, & all the many chinks in it admitted the air & the cold from all sides freely: so that my Situation became every day more unfavourable, at the increasingly cold weather.

He tried hard not to show his discomfort to his shipmates, but it was not easy and even the thought of his £4,000 did little to lift his spirits:

I put on a good face, & wanted to shew a mind superior to all these inconveniences & hardships, but had my Shipmates had a Sight into my most private thoughts they would have me found widely different, from what I wanted to appear: & indeed I must confess, if twice 4000 pounds were offerred to me to go again on such a Voyage, & go through all the

Scenes I was obliged to pass now: I would willingly give Up this great inducement & which is so powerfull with many, & exchange it as willingly with the necessity of writing & working very hard for the Support of myself & my Family: & after all, I had, when I left England a fair prospect of getting a place at the Brittish Museum, my friends having interested themselves very much in my favour, & obtained the promiss of His Grace the Archbishop & of the Speaker of the House of Commons; this place & a little industry would have kept me from want & necessity. Had it not been, for the pleasing hopes of making great discoveries in Natural History in this Expedition, I would never had so great an Inclination of going on it. But instead of meeting with any object worthy of our attention, after having circumnavigated very near half the globe, we saw nothing, but water. Ice & sky: &; what casts another damp on my Spirits: the Capt throws hints out of staying all the winter in Queen Charlotte's Sound, a cold place under barren rocks, without having any refreshments from the Tropical fruits, a place where all plants will be killed by the blasting cold of the winds pouring down from Mountains covered with Snow: without fish, birds or any other Animals, either for supplying us with fresh food or to afford employment for the Naturalist.[12]

There was little of interest to the naturalists: there no sign of land and the icebergs carried no vegetation – there were seabirds and penguins, but this leg of the voyage was barren as regarded botanising. There were small consolations: the chronometer was keeping good time, the general health of the crew and the freedom from scurvy was remarkable considering that they had been fifteen weeks in the Antarctic seas, in the worst and coldest conditions imaginable.

For another four weeks, the *Resolution* sailed along the edge of the ice sheet at about the sixtieth parallel until she had gained sufficient westerly to head northwards towards New Zealand. A great expanse of southerly ocean had been explored. The passage from Cape Town to New Zealand covered a staggering 157 degrees of longitude. There was the great achievement of entering the Antarctic Circle – though there was no land and the whole passage had been one of incredible hardship and endurance. It was with great relief on 26 March 1773 that the westernmost cape of New Zealand was sighted from the masthead. It was a dangerous and rocky coast on which to find a landing and it was still a few days' sail from the arranged rendezvous at the other end of the South Island, but Cook knew it was essential to land as soon as possible and rest his weary men.

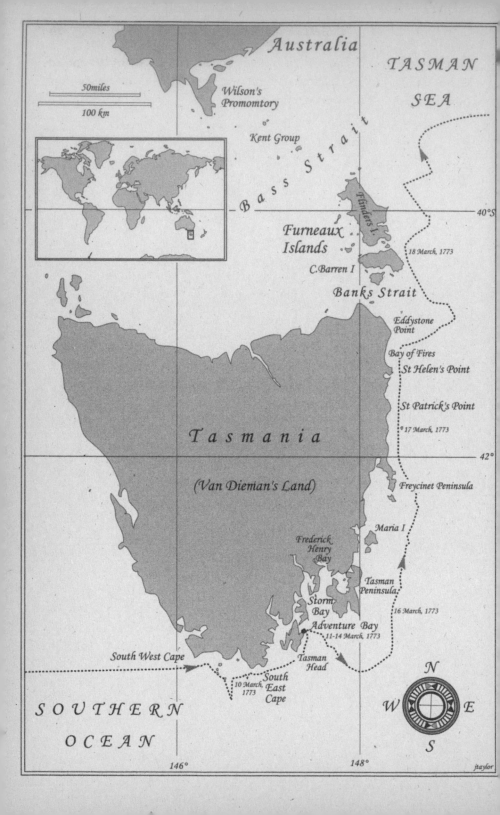

FOUR

The Rendezvous

Meanwhile the heavens revolved and night swept over the sea,
embracing in deep darkness both earth and sky.

Aeneid, ii, 251

The situation aboard the *Adventure* was very similar to that on board
the *Resolution*. The report of the gun was heard, but it was more distant
than expected. The fog was very thick and they estimated *Resolution* to
be about three miles away. *Adventure* fired her own gun in answer. After
a time, some thought there seemed to be a reply but it was even
more distant than before. They fired every half hour until four in the
afternoon, but there was no further response. At five o'clock the fog
cleared and one of the seaman thought he could see the *Resolution* on the
horizon. They scurried to set the sails and head towards the sighting. It
was of no avail and no ship appeared on the skyline. The next day, the
fog returned and the *Adventure* continued firing a gun every half hour
but there was still no reply. They had to face the cold truth that the
two ships were parted. Like Cook, Captain Furneaux spent one more
day searching aimlessly, and then he decided to execute the contingency
plan.

The rendezvous at Queen Charlotte Sound in New Zealand would
be easy enough to find. One of the Arnold watches was keeping good
time and they had the astronomer Bayly on board to help find the ship's
position. In any case they had Cook's chart of New Zealand and it was
just a matter of finding the west coast and following it in the right
direction. Furneaux reasoned that Tasman, in 1642, had sailed these
same seas at a latitude of about forty degrees. He knew that Cook
would be sailing at the high latitudes so he chose to work his way a few

degrees to the north and sail a mid course at a more tolerable fifty-two degrees south. Then he headed northwards in search of the land that had been discovered by Tasman 130 years ago – the place he had called Van Dieman's Land.

The sea was almost clear of icebergs and everything went according to plan. It was the end of February and the nights were still short, but the skies were clear and a very bright meteor was sighted to the north, heading in a southwesterly direction. They were also treated to a magnificent display of the southern lights, the aurora australis, that lasted for several consecutive nights. The lights appeared as a set of white streaks in the sky radiating from a point some distance away from the zenith. The astronomer William Bayly was particularly impressed by the display: it was the first time on the voyage that the lights had been seen and they were so bright that he claimed he 'could read common good print very distinct'. The display was also seen from the *Resolution* and George Forster gave an excellent description dated 17 February. He claimed that they differed in some respects from the northern lights:

A beautiful phenomenon was observed during the preceding night, which appeared again this and several following nights. It consisted of long columns of a clear white light, shooting up from the horizon to the eastward, almost to the zenith, and gradually spreading on the whole southern part of the sky. These columns were sometime bent sideways at their upper extremity, and though in most respects similar to the northern lights (aurora borealis) of our hemisphere, yet differed from them, in being always of a whitish colour whereas ours assume various tints, especially those of a fiery purple hue. The stars were sometime hid by, and sometime faintly to be seen through the substance of these southern lights, but never had the fiery appearance sometimes seen in Sweden.[1]

On 1 March, there was a cry of land. It was a false alarm caused by a cloud formation. The loneliness of the long voyage was telling on the crew and a few days after the false alarm one of the midshipmen, George Moorey, experienced what he thought was a supernatural occurrence when he was serving his lone watch on the forecastle. He saw a vision of his father standing near him on the quarterdeck, dressed in the clothing he wore in England when they parted company before the voyage. Moorey ran to the rear of the ship in a great state of agitation, he was convinced that his father had died on the other side of the planet and that his ghost had made an appearance to him.

On 9 March, however, land *was* sighted and there was no doubt that the *Adventure* was approaching Van Dieman's Land. Furneaux gave his first impressions:

> On the 9th of March, little wind and pleasent weather, about 9AM, being then in the Latitude 43°37' South, Longitude by lunar observation 145°36' East and by Account 143°10' East a Greenwich, we saw the Land bearing NNE about 8 or 9 Leagues distance; it appeared moderately high, and uneven near the sea, the hill further back formed a double Land and much higher, there seemed to be several islands broken land to the NW as the shore trenched, but by the reason of Clouds that hung over them could not be certain whether they did not join to the main, we hauled immediately up for it and by noon within 3 or 4 leagues of it, a point much like the Ramhead off Plymouth, which I take to be the same Tasman calls South Cape, bore North four leagues of us, the Land from this cape runs directly to the Eastward. About four Leagues alongshore there are Three Islands about two miles long and several rocks resembling the Mewstone (particularly one which we so named) about four or five leagues ESE ½ E off the above Cape that Tasman has not mentioned, nor laid down in his draughts.[2]

Cook's biographers have not been generous in describing this early event in Tasmanian history. It is true that on his second voyage Cook did not personally land in the country which became known as Tasmania and it is also true that the land was not a new discovery. Cook was the leader of the expedition, however, and the *Adventure* was the first British ship ever to sight Van Dieman's Land. A French ship had landed in Tasmania in the previous year under the command of Marion du Fresne, but the French were interested only in repairs and fresh water. The descriptions from the *Adventure* are therefore of great value, with only Tasman's and a brief French account to precede them. Furneaux, although he had access to the record of Tasman's voyage, had great difficulty trying to relate his findings to those of the earlier explorer. There were so many small islands offshore from the mainland that it was difficult to identify those described by Tasman. Tobias

Furneaux looked for a safe place to land behind the islands. He sent
out one of the ship's boats but after only about half an hour the weather
conditions deteriorated so badly that he fired a signal for the boat to
return. It thus chanced that the honour of being the first Englishman
to set foot on Tasmanian soil fell to Dr Burney's son, the second
lieutenant, who was put in charge of the large cutter on the second
landing attempt. As with the earlier attempt, the seas roughened soon
after the boat was out of sight of the ship and again Furneaux sounded
his guns to call the cutter back. This time, he was too late. The surf
ran high on the beach and Burney's party could not hear the signal
above the breakers. With some difficulty, they made a landing at a place
which became known as Louisa Bay:

> at $\frac{1}{2}$ past 6 we passd a fine deep Bay with Several Islands in it – there are
> two pretty high peaks just to the Eastward of it – at 9 The Large Cutter
> was hoisted out & I was sent in her to see if I could find any fresh water
> we row'd in Shore a little to the Eastward of the Bay just mention'd. We
> Observd the Land seemed to part which made me conjecture there was
> a fresh Water River there – I would gladly have gone to have Seen but
> it was too far from the Ship – by 11 we got in a Small Bay where we saw
> a Sandy beach but could not Land there for the Surf – however we found
> a good Landing place on some Rocks. The first thing we Saw when we
> climbd up was Some Wood Ashes the remains of a Fire which had been
> kindled there & a great Number of Scollop Shells – We saw none of the
> Inhabitants – there was a path leading through the Woods which would
> probably have led us to some of their Huts – but we could not stay to
> walk up the Wind coming too fresh Obligd us to think of getting on
> board again[3]

In the boat with James Burney was midshipman John Wilby, who gives
a less lucid account than Burney, but he adds a few details of the
landing:

> Hoisted out the Large Cutter and sent her in Shore in search of fresh
> water, with our 2nd Lieut a Mate and Midshipman, with 7 hands arm'd.
> We Row'd in Shore to the E[ast]ward of the Bay just Mention'd [Cox
> Bight] where we Observ'd the Land to part, we conjectured a fresh
> water River was there, But being too far from the Ship, we row'd into a
> Small Bay to the E[ast]ward where we attemp'd to Land on a Sandy
> Beach but could not for the Surf. However we Land a Little to right of

it, under the Lee of some Rocks that Projectured out. We climb'd up
these Rocks inadvertantly without our Arm's, But on Reccolection by
the Sight of Wood Ashes, we procured our Implemts and proceed'd in
our Attempt. We Observ'd a Path Leading in the Wood which had we
followd, would in all Probability Led us to the Natives, but the Weathr
growing Hazy and Likely to Blow, we took the Prudentest Method, of
Returng on Board; Haveg takg a convinceg proof of their Being natives
near [at] hand. at the Larbd Hand comeg out their is a fine Run of Water
from the Rocks, but not safe, too near it in a Boat: $\frac{1}{2}$ past 12 got Safe on
Board to the great Joy of our Shipmates: They haveg Fired Serv[era]l
Guns as Sigls for us, which we heard nothing Off. The Ship was under
Close Reef Topsls and the Weathr Grew very dirty – Its very Bold
in Shore, haveg many Bays; and the Land coverd with Trees, makg
every[where] an Entire Wood.[4]

James Burney went on to describe other signs of habitation. They could
see no inhabitants; he concluded that there were probably no aborigines
in the vicinity and that the site had been abandoned for several months.
But there were fires on the north side of the bay, where the land was
lower and there were less trees and apparently no undergrowth. There
were a few huts, some hollowed-out trees and overgrown pathways
leading into the woods:

The place did not seem to have been inhabited for some months before,
so that it was not our coming frightend them away – it is most likely
the Natives never stay long in one place but lead a Wandring life,
travelling along the coast from Bay to Bay to catch fish which by the
great quantities of shells we Saw, must make the chief part of their food –
Their Huts are very low and ill contrivd, & seem only intended for
Temporary habitations: they had left nothing in them but 2 or 3 Old
baskets or bags made of a very strong grass –, Some flint & tinder which
I believe they make of the bark of a Tree, & a great number of pearl
Scollop, Mussel, Lobster & Cray fish Shells which they had roasted.[5]

Captain Furneaux was very concerned for the safety of his crew
members and he was relieved to see them return to the ship later in
the day. The bay provided a safe anchorage, however, and also a supply
of fresh water, and he therefore decided to bring the ship in and stop
for a short time. He thought at first that he had landed in Frederick
Henry Bay, where Tasman had landed before him, but eventually he

realised that the bay did not fit Tasman's description. He called the place Adventure Bay, although in fact it is thought to have been the bay described by Tasman as Storm Bay. James Burney's narrative goes on to describe the wildlife in the area. The lagoons and lakes were abundant with fish, and the trees were full of colourful birds, including a magnificent white eagle. There was at least one sighting of a possum. On the downside, there were the giant Tasmanian stinging ants which they encountered for the first time:

> This Land is situated in a fine temperate & healthy Climate – the Country is exceeding pleasant, but it is almost impossible to penetrate into it on account of the Woods. Here are some small snakes, one of which we caught, & a great Number of very large Ants about an Inch & a half long – they bite very sharp & are exceeding troublesome – The Trees are mostly Evergreens, standing very thick and close together – many of the Small ones bore berries of a spicy flavour – the larger ones are in general quite Strait & Shoot up very high before they branch out. They are large enough for Masts for any Ship in the Navy, but are rather brittle and heavy – they have a Soft thick bark which many of them had been strippd of by the Natives – the Wood is of a reddish cast & has a great deal of gum in it – at the back of some of the Sandy beaches are Small Lagoons or Lakes with good Store of Trout, Carp, & other Fish – here is likewise plenty of wild fowl & game but so Shy that I imagine the Natives have some method of catching them – We Shot some Wild Ducks, Crows, Parroquets, a White Eagle & some Small birds.[6]

He described the eagle as one of the noblest birds he had ever seen. There were tracks made by wild beasts and the dung of a large mammal. One of the party shot a catlike animal which was probably a possum. It was the only mammal they saw. The landing party climbed high enough to look across the bay. An expanse of water could be seen beyond, though they could not decide whether it was an arm of the sea or an inland lagoon. James Burney thought that it could be the Bay of Frederick Henry, discovered by Tasman, but this was mere speculation. There was land again beyond the water and fertile country to the north, where the smoke from many fires implied that it was well inhabited. No contact had been made with the native people. This may have been a result of their shyness, but it seems more likely that they were simply not in the area at the time. They might have opposed the landing on their territory or they might have welcomed the visitors – all this is mere speculation.

It was time to return to the ship and they left behind a small cask, several medals tied to the trees and a few other items of small value. Burney, knowing nothing of the recent landing by the French, wondered at being the first European to see Van Dieman's Land since it was first discovered 130 years previously. There is no specific mention of a kangaroo, but Bayly mentions plentiful dung 'in hard buttons' which may be taken as evidence of their presence near the landing place. Once again, Burney's account of Tasmania is supported by midshipman John Wilby, who describes the signs of human habitation and the shyness of the Tasmanian aborigines who they knew were not very far away. He tells a little of the wildlife, and describes a gum tree with a girth of twenty-six feet:

This day we Found out Sevl Huts or Wigwams with some Bags in them, made of weed But not the Least Appearance of any People. They have nothing to Live on but Shellfish, that we can Observe, for the Birds, what Few there are, is so shy, that its difficult to get a Shot at them. To the sw of the First Waterg Place there is a Large Lagoon which I believe has Plenty of Fish in it for one of our Gentlemen caught upwards of 2 Dozen Trout, and Shot a Possum, which was the only Animal we saw. Their are a great many Gum Trees and of a vast Thickness and Hight, one of Which Measured in Circumference 26 feet & ye Height under the Branches was 20 feet. The Tree seems most of 'em to have been Burnt down, for their was not the Least Appearance of any Ingenuitty. We see their Fires in a Sandy Bay to the N[orth]ward of us, but no way Inclineable to near us But seem'd rather to Fly From us.[7]

When he had completed the re-watering of his ship, Furneaux decided not to stay any longer and on 15 March he weighed anchor and sailed northwards, mapping and charting the east coast of Tasmania. St Patrick's Head was sighted and named on St Patrick's Day. St Helen's Point was named the following day. They sailed northwards and soon there was a great swell from the west, which carried the *Adventure* out to sea and away from the land. To the north, another cape was visible, and Furneaux thought he had passed a deep bay but did not sail in close enough to explore and chart it. He passed two large islands, now called Barren Island and Flinders Island. He guessed correctly that they were separated from the mainland but did not stop to investigate closer, yet the island group became known as the Furneaux Islands. At this point, the *Adventure* was only about two days' sail from Cook's first sighting of the east coast of New Holland, and this is where we discover that Tobias Furneaux was no James Cook. He found open sea to the north but he concluded that Van Dieman's Land and New Holland were the same landmass and that there existed a deep bay connecting his northernmost cape with Cook's sighting on the Australian mainland. He did not sail to the north or the west to confirm his hypothesis.

It was obvious that Furneaux had reached a premature conclusion. Midshipman Richard Hergest noted that 'All the land we have passed this Afternoon [18 March] Appeared to be a Number of Islands if so they are Strong Confirmation of the Supposed Streights & are in the Mouth of it between Van Dieman's land and New Holland.' James Burney also thought there was a strait, as did Arthur Kempe, the first lieutenant, although the latter was more cautious: 'The opening which we discovered on the 19th Inst I take to be the Streights leading between New Holland and Van Dieman's land, but this is mere conjecture, as we were not nigh enough to be certain, whether there is a straight leading thro or not.'

It is easy to be wise after the event, but it was not until the following century, and long after the First Fleet landed at Botany Bay, that the Lincolnshire explorers George Bass and Matthew Flinders first proved that a strait existed between Australia and Tasmania. It seems incredible that the early ships to Port Jackson could have saved up to two weeks' sailing time if they had known about the existence of the Bass Straits, but the straits remained undiscovered for another generation. On Friday 19 March (1773) the *Adventure* left the north-east corner of Tasmania and set course for New Zealand.

There were a few problems on board the *Adventure*. James Scott, lieutenant of the marines, was insolent towards the captain and he was thrown out of the great cabin with the door slammed behind him. 'He was of an unhappy temper always quarrelling with the captain and officers,' said the astronomer Bayly. 'He being a great stickler for *honour*, that if you spoke the least word in a joke his scotch blood would be up.'

Perhaps the astronomer was melodramatic, but Bayly also described a second incident during the passage from Van Dieman's Land to New Zealand. The lieutenants Kempe and Burney, Andrews the surgeon and midshipman Hawkey all came hammering on Bayly's door asking for brandy. It was after midnight and they had all been drinking. Bayly claimed that they had a hammer and chisel and that they began taking his door off its hinges. The astronomer pulled on his clothes and took Burney by the collar, forcing him down on the arms chest. Then they all came running after him, with the surgeon waving a hammer. Was this no more than too much alcohol and high jinks? Tobias Furneaux, to his credit, heard the scuffle and soon put a stop to it.

The tomfoolery may have been all in jest, but there were more serious problems on board the *Adventure* – there were several outbreaks of scurvy. Furneaux did not apply the strict dietary measures insisted upon by Cook. It was fortunate for him that he sighted New Zealand only two weeks after leaving Van Dieman's Land and he had no trouble in finding the rendezvous. He then had the means to obtain fresh food and vegetables. He went some way towards redeeming himself: he quickly set up trade with the Maoris and started to cultivate crops. There could be little doubt that they were at the right place. James Burney discovered a place where the *Endeavour* had watered, and here he found the names of some of the men carved on the trees.

By the time the *Adventure* reached the rendezvous, the *Resolution* was already anchored in another part of New Zealand, at the opposite end of the South Island. The west coast of New Zealand's South Island is amongst the most formidable in the southern hemisphere. Three years earlier, Cook had refused to risk his ship on this coast when Joseph Banks had been keen to land and botanise. This was one of the reasons why Banks wanted to be in charge of any future expeditions and it was also one of the reasons why the Admiralty did not want laymen to have command of their ships. In 1773, however, the need to make a landing was much greater than before. The sailors on the *Resolution* had been sixteen weeks in some of the most severe weather conditions on earth. Cook therefore took a calculated risk and headed for a broken inlet, which he called Dusky Sound. He was fortunate: the inlet was part of a sea passage around an island which became known as Resolution

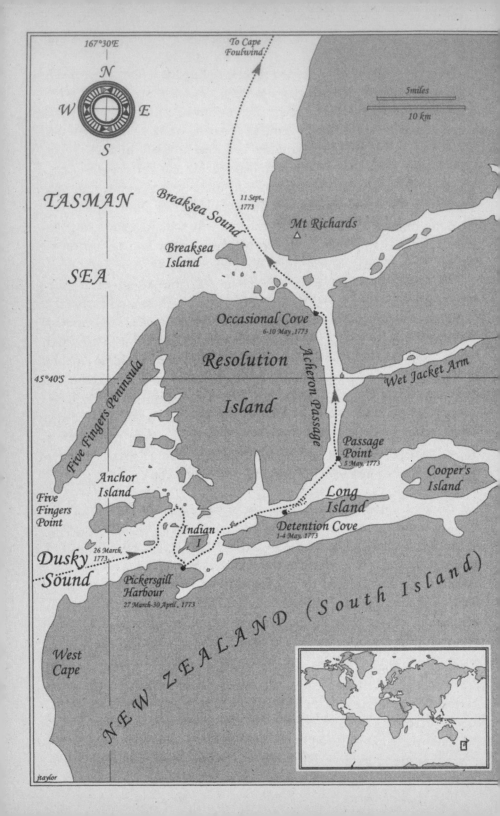

Island. It had sheltered water behind, welcome greenery, fresh running water and fuel for the ship. He had just one human case of scurvy, but most of the surviving animals were in a dreadful condition. Only two sheep and one or two goats were still alive and they were suffering badly from lack of fresh food. The ship's cat and Forster's dog both had raw gums and loose teeth and were suffering from advanced stages of the disease. One of the first priorities was to find the best place to anchor the ship. Cook set off to explore the north side of the Sound whilst Pickersgill explored the south. Pickersgill was the more fortunate. He found the better harbour and it was named after him. There was a convenient tree growing out almost horizontally over the water; this was used as a gangplank and the artist William Hodges found this natural bridge of sufficient interest to paint a picture of it.

Dusky Sound was a welcome and impressive haven after the icy seas of the Antarctic. The cliffs rose sheer from the sea to a height of several hundred feet, the tops frequently hidden in the mist. The height of the ship's masts was nothing in comparison with the cliffs and the *Resolution* was dwarfed by the grand works of nature. Vegetation clung to every possible nook and cranny, all the land at the foot of the cliffs was heavily wooded and a sparkling white cascade of fresh water fell continually from a great height near the little harbour. Anders Sparrman recorded his first impressions:

> During our passage of nine or ten miles through the beautiful archipelago of Dusky Bay, I looked as a botanist most eagerly at the green veil of Flora: but, from the tops of the mountains down to their utmost foot by the edge of the sea, there was a dense covering of thickets and trees, foliage and pine-needles, and in such profusion that not the smallest patch was left for further adornment by green grass and plants.
>
> Already some of the foliferous trees seemed to have assumed their autumn dress with an exhibition of yellow leaves, yet this did not make an unpleasant variation in the green picture; little waterfalls and brooks, peeping forth here and there from the mountains towards the sunlight, crystal clear and shining silver, could hardly fail to make a most lovely effect. At this sight, the seamen decided that they would have an easy and sufficient supply of the most vital of all needs they look for in harbour for their ship, fresh water, which is also the chief essential for the luxury of grog and punch.

Enormous mast-trees raised their cedar-like tops proudly and majestically high above the other tall trees in the valleys; the flight of seabirds and pelicans along the shores, and the various chirpings and pleasant songs of the land-birds in the nearby dells, enlivened the whole scene. What a heavenly contrast to storms, cold, ice, and the occasional scream of a penguin in a boundless Antarctic sea![8]

Seaward of Resolution Island was Five Fingers Peninsula, so named because the continuous beating of the sea had sculptured it to bear a resemblance to a huge human hand. The botany and wildlife was so abundant that the Forsters, even with the help of Anders Sparrman, did not have the time to do it justice. The fish were so plentiful that in a few hours one boat could catch enough to feed the whole crew. The trees, growing tall and straight and sound, were excellent for replacing ship's masts, worn spars, the decking and other timbers. It was marvellous to be back on land again, and at night they were serenaded by a chorus of singing birds. The birds were so tame that they seemed ready to settle on a man's hand or on his head or the barrel of his gun – it seems cruel that the naturalists shot the birds to take as specimens and the sailors did the same to supplement the crew's fresh food supplies. The ship's cat went foraging every day and could not believe its luck to find birds that had never before experienced a cat. The wildfowl supply was so plentiful that the few surviving geese, who had travelled all the way from Cape Town, were given the freedom of New Zealand.

The extreme south of New Zealand was not as thickly populated as the north, but there was a small party of Maoris in the vicinity and they were soon discovered by a hunting party, about a mile away from the ship with their canoes. The Maoris were shy but inquisitive. The next day, they came nearer but still remained wary of what to them seemed an alien invasion from a world far beyond their experience. Cook wanted to befriend them, and it is here that we find the classic textbook image of Captain Cook making contact with the natives. Forster and Elliott give very similar accounts:

When we were about a mile & a half from the Ship, we were haled from the point of a rock, & when we looked at it we found the voices came from some Natives, one of which stood on the top of a projecting rock.

We stood in towards the rock & called to him *hallemaiu Tayo*, come here Friend: but he did not stir; now & then he spoke seemingly with violence & threatened with his staff of honour, upon which he leaned. Capt Cook went to the head of the boat & called him friendly & threw him his handkerchief & I gave him myne likewise. Capt Cook took two sheets of white paper & went on the rock, handed it to the Native, who was then trembling; he took it however & laid it on the rock before him. Then Capt Cook handed both handkerchiefs to him, which he likewise laid down: then Capt Cook shook hands with him, & lastly went up to him & nosed him, which is the mark of friendship among these people. Then Capt Cook pointed at two young people that stood at a distance with lances, that they should lay them down, but the old man misunderstood it & called them; they came both: one of them had on the upperlip a monstrous wen or excrescence; they were both females. The old man had a very fine countenance. The one girl looked not disagreable, & soon began to chatter away in her language, like a magpie.[9]

Where Forster found the girl 'not disagreeable', John Elliott paid her the compliment of 'the finest woman we saw in this country' and he estimated her height as five feet, eight or nine inches. William Wales recorded that one of the marines, who must have been Samuel Gibson because he knew a little of the language, actually asked the father for her hand in marriage. The man was taken aback and begged time to consult his God. The Maori family was still very wary of the newcomers, but Cook worked hard at gaining their confidence and soon they began to respond to his approaches. The family consisted of a man with two 'wives': the elder wife seemed to be the mother of the younger wife. There was a boy of fourteen or fifteen and three young children, the youngest still sucking at his mother's breast. William Hodges made a drawing of the Maoris and called them the Toetoe family. There was much that they did not understand about the strangers and much that the strangers did not understand about them.

The Maoris were still afraid to go near the ship and they refused Cook's offer to enter the cabin. He persevered with them, however, and the marines gave a performance on bagpipes, fife and drum and eventually the elderly man and the girl were persuaded to come on to the deck. The girl was obviously fascinated by everything she saw, and in time she lost her inhibitions, chatting incessantly in her native language. She deliberately stroked the poor ship's cat in the wrong direction. She enjoyed the attention of the strangers and when she relaxed she was so thrilled with her new experiences that she treated the men to a dance on the deck of the ship. As she gained more confidence, she paid a lot of attention to one of the younger crew members because she thought he was her own sex – but when she discovered her mistake, she was embarrassed and wanted no more to do with him. One of the young officers jokingly offered to shoot the man who had offended her, but the girl sat between her mother and father and burst into tears. The journals do not tell us the name of the sailor, but the younger men such as Elliott and Hood are likely candidates, or possibly George Vancouver – all three would have been too young to have grown a beard. John Elliott was the most likely of the three, for we know from his journal that he was very taken by her. Having recovered from her mistake with the younger man, the artist William Hodges became her favourite – probably because she understood and liked his paintings, which included a picture of her own family. 'When the girl saw Mr Hodges she began to frisk with him, & threw the coat or mat she intended to give him over his shoulders; & wanted to tie his hairs up on the crown of his head,' wrote Forster.

The *Resolution* stayed six weeks at Dusky Sound. The temporary settlement acquired an observatory for William Wales to make his observations, a forge for the working of metals, a hut for the wood-cutters and carpenters, a pen for the sheep and over an acre of cleared ground reclaimed from the trees – some of it sown for crops. There were a few short expeditions, but these were of limited scope because the anchorage was hemmed in by cliffs. It was the rainy season and when the rains came they poured down in great abundance, swelling the force of the nearby cascade. Forster took a boat to take a closer look at the waterfall, a sight with 'more beauty and grandeur than any thing, I had hitherto seen'. He estimated that the column of water, gushing out of the rock in a great torrent, was between six to eight yards in circumference and it fell a full one hundred yards before striking a steep sloping rock. The water spread out to a sheet of twenty-five yards in width, the bulk of which was collected in a basin about sixty feet in circumference. For a hundred yards around the cataract there was a watery mist. Forster climbed some way up the fall and there, with the roaring of the falling water all around him, he looked down at the basin as the sun came out behind him. He saw a beautiful bright rainbow in the water droplets, covering not simply an arc but a full circle with a secondary bow outside it. William Wales also saw the waterfall and was moved to quote from James Thomson's *The Seasons*:

> Smooth to the shelving brink a copious flood
> Roll'd fir, and placid; where collected all,
> In one impetuous torrent, down the Steep
> It thundering shot, and shook the country round.
> At first an azure sheet; it rushed broad;
> Then whitening by degrees, as prone it fell,
> And from the loud resounding Rocks below
> Dash'd in a cloud of foam, it sent aloft
> A hoary mist, in which Sol's lucid beams
> Refracted, formed a triple coloured bow.[10]

James Thomson (1700–48)

Meals were often eaten in the open air, seated at a roaring fireside, with abundance of fresh water from the stream and kegs of spruce beer to quench the thirst. In contrast to the violent boxing matches, the sailors were at their best in this relaxed situation, exchanging yarns and anecdotes with jokes and comic adventures. Forster gives an interesting account of the men from the lower decks enjoying their fare:

> Whilst the Officers & Better people eat their meal, the Sailors dress theirs & give way to mirth & jollity & crack jokes, wherein if you observe a good deal of genius, & good nature, blended with roughness, bluntness, hearty curses, oaths & baudy expressions. Often I heard very smart repartees, witticisms & jokes from the mouth of an honest tar that would have done honour to the greatest genius of the age; & their stories though for the most part bawdy & indelicate are often as chaste as possible . . .[11]

Cook himself liked to explore the inlets, but while he took the greatest pains to look after the health of his crew, he neglected his own. He would wade through the shallow water, getting thoroughly soaked in the process, and then he would sit in the boat in his wet clothing. It was not just the creeks and rivulets that caused the soakings. At times, the rain was incessant. The creek called Wetjacket Arm, for example, was named after a shooting expedition from which every member returned to the ship with clothing wet through from the rain. In his younger years, Cook's robust health could easily take this kind of punishment, but now that he was in his mid-forties, he had a price to pay for his own neglect. He contracted a fever and a pain in the groin, which terminated in a rheumatic swelling of the right foot. Cook complained of what he called a 'cold', which prevented him from exploring ahead of the ship to find a safe passage. Forster did not agree with his Captain's diagnosis. He thought that the captain was very ill and he over-reacted, fearing the very worst:

> ... I am sorry for the Capt who in this bad weather ventured out with an ill health, & a bad foot, which might throw him in a disease & make all on board unhappy, for the very thought, that the first Lieut should then command the Ship if the Capt should die, is enough to frighten every living soul in the same; as none is a stranger to his illtemper, capricious & whimsical way of thinking, without any principles.[12]

Forster's remarks about Robert Cooper, the first lieutenant, should be read in conjunction with a comment by the astronomer William Wales, who wrote that: 'Before we reached New Zealand the first time, there was scarce a man in the ship with whom he [J. R. Forster] had not quarrelled with on one pretence or another.' Forster was an excellent botanist, but he was not a sailor; he was not used to the harsh conditions on board a ship of His Majesty's Navy.

Cook explored along the creek where the ship was anchored and discovered that it entered the sea again about twelve miles to the north. The straits were wide enough and the passage was deep enough to take the ship and he decided to depart by this route. He soon found that he had made an error of judgement and reaching the Tasman Sea took him far longer than he had anticipated. At first, he was becalmed and was obliged to anchor until the wind picked up. The weather refused to change and the ship's boats were therefore put out to tow her laboriously along the passage. The next day, a light wind sprung up which promised to assist them and they seemed to make good progress, but it died away quickly and they found that because of tide and current they had lost more headway than they had gained. Then came very bad weather, with a violent storm accompanied by snow, hail and thunder. The *Resolution* had to shelter in a small cove and was confined to the inlet until the storms abated. Much of the time, it was possible to explore the neighbouring creeks and to return with game for the next meal. It was eleven days before the *Resolution* finally gained the open sea, but once she was clear of the land, she made good progress. Cape Foulwind lived up to its name and held up progress for a time, but soon Cape Farewell was sighted, the point where the *Endeavour* had left New Zealand in 1770. Ship Cove in Queen Charlotte Sound was not far away.

On Monday 17 May, at about four in the afternoon, they were off the broken islands on the approach to the rendezvous when a number of water spouts were spotted. This was a common enough phenomenon in the seas around New Zealand and they did not normally present any danger. Six or seven were seen in all. All but one of them died away quickly, but the largest spout remained; it was a huge and powerful column of water reaching right up to the clouds and estimated to be about sixty feet in diameter at its base. It was a small tornado. The motion of the spout was erratic, but it was obviously getting closer and if it hit the ship the masts and superstructure would be destroyed like matchwood. The water spout came within fifty feet of the stern. The crew watched with great consternation, but the crisis passed by and, greatly to the relief of all on board, it wandered off in a different direction.

The next day, the ship was six leagues east of Cape Farewell when Cook noted a spacious bay, which he rightly concluded was called Murderer's Bay. Here, Tasman lost four men when he landed in 1642. Soon the ship was abreast of Cape Jackson and they saw a welcome sight: it was the flash of two guns followed by low, distant thunder, which could only come from their sister ship, the *Adventure*. Soon, the *Adventure*'s boat under command of Lieutenant Kempe was coming out to greet them, the wind had dropped and they needed a tow to make progress. The *Resolution* dropped anchor in Ship Cove and Captain Furneaux came aboard to exchange news and reports.

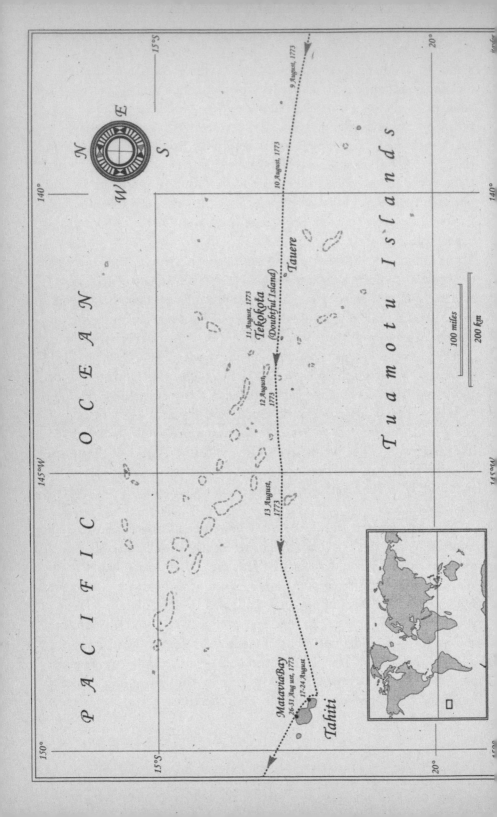

FIVE

Tropical Interlude

The south wind stretches our sails: we flee over the foaming waves where the wind and the helmsman called the course.

Aeneid, III, 268

'Both ships felt an uncommon joy at our meeting after an absence of fourteen weeks,' said Furneaux. The crews of both the *Resolution* and the *Adventure* were delighted to have made a successful rendezvous in the southern hemisphere. Tobias Furneaux came on board to be greeted by Cook and they exchanged gossip and accounts of their separate journeys. Cook was pleased enough with the *Adventure*'s achievements; he carefully scrutinised the log and asked many questions about Van Dieman's Land. He seems to have accepted Furneaux's theory that he had landed on the coast of New Holland and that Van Dieman's Land was not a separate island. However, he did not spend much time discussing the matter with Kempe and Burney, both of whom thought Van Dieman's Land to be separate from New Holland: otherwise, he might well have decided to investigate for himself. He decided not to return to the west but to explore the seas to the east of New Zealand. In some respects, Furneaux had done well. He had planted vegetables, released a boar and a sow to breed in the wild and built up a good trade for food and supplies with the Maoris. He was a good captain, a fine seaman, he commanded respect from officers and seamen and he kept discipline. He seems to fall short on exploration and on his failure to contain scurvy, but these are things of which he had little experience and it is perhaps unfair to compare him to James Cook, who was the greatest captain of all time when it came to exploration and discovery.

The Maoris placed great store by glass bottles, and they also wanted nails and hatchets, for which they would trade fish and supplies. They refused wine and spirits, for which they had yet to acquire a taste, but they liked water sweetened with sugar. They saw beads, ribbons and other trinkets as being of no use to them and therefore of no value. Cook, with great difficulty, had managed to keep his last ram and ewe alive through the terrible Antarctic passage. He released them to a well-earned retirement with the optimistic hope that they would give birth to the New Zealand lamb industry. The green grass of New Zealand should have quickly restored them, but, alas, it did not agree with their digestive system and in a few days both the sheep died. He also released a male and female goat, thinking that they would survive well in the mountainous terrain.

The Maoris at Queen Charlotte Sound, who well remembered Captain Cook and the *Endeavour* from three years ago, asked after Tupia, the Tahitian who had made a great impression on them because he had been able to converse freely with them in their own language. Cook had to explain that Tupia had died on the journey to England. The Maoris were dismayed and they even went as far as to compose and sing a memorial song for him. The Maoris readily boarded both ships to trade, and although they sometimes coveted the men's shirts and jackets or the ship's table linen, they generally accepted the situation when they were refused. Johann Forster gives an account of a skirmish between a sailor and a Maori when a jacket had been stolen and it had to be recovered by force, but this seems to have been the exception rather than the rule. However, one Maori stole a copy of Fielding's *Tom Jones* from the cabin of a midshipman.

On one occasion, a Maori brought his small son on board the ship and pushed him forward for inspection. The British thought the man was offering the child for sale and they wanted nothing to do with him, but because of the language problem they misunderstood the father's intention. He wanted the British to give the boy a present. Cook gladly gave a shirt, and the boy pranced happily around the ship in his new garment, but this prompted a little jealousy from some quarters. Old Will, the ship's goat, butted the boy in the backside and soiled the new shirt. The boy was afraid to show it to his father but the seamen kindly washed it for him before sending him home. Forster also recorded an occasion when the Maoris did a dance on the quarterdeck: they lined up in a row and the leader sang a few words and began to make motions with his arms. They all followed him in his motions, extending one hand and then the other and stamping with their feet. They repeated the words of the song and there seemed to be some sort of rhyme to it, but none of the British was able to work it out fully. The best description of the Maori music, as might be expected, comes from the pen of James Burney:

> As yet I have not mentioned their Music. I shall say but little on this subject for very little will suffice, their Instruments are Flutes & Trumpets – the flutes are more curious for their carving than for any Music that can be got out of them. I shall bring home a Specimen, the Trumpet is a Tube about 7 feet long – they make these & the flutes by getting a piece of wood fit for their purpose. They then shape it on the outside & afterwoods split it in 2. These parts being hollowd are woulded [sic] together & are sure to fit exactly. I saw but one of their Trumpets the whole time we staid here & that Captn Furneaux got – the notes on this vary according as you blow more or less. I question whether a man who understands the French horn might not be able to play a Tune on it – as to the Zealanders they constantly sounded the same Note. Tasman mentions one of these Instruments in his account of Murderers Bay – The Zealanders commonly give us a Song when they leave the Ship – there is no great variety in the Music, however it comes nearer to a Tune than anything I have heard here – the words I neither understood nor can remember – here is the Tune they keep singing the 2 first Bars till their words are expended & then close with the last – Sometimes they Sing an underpart which is a third lower except the 2 last notes which are the same.[1]

On 5 June 1773 the British patriotically celebrated the King's birthday. Forster was particularly pleased with the ceremony because he valued the German connections with the House of Hanover, but we wonder what the Maoris made of a twenty-one-gun salute fired for reasons they could not understand. This was all part of a relaxed interlude, but Tobias Furneaux was in for an unpleasant surprise. He had naturally assumed that he and his crew could take their ease in New Zealand for the duration of the southern winter, but he soon found that Captain Cook had no such plans. Cook well knew that if he outstayed his welcome the Maoris could become restless and he also knew that it would be inviting problems for his own men to remain idle for too long. There was far more ocean yet to be covered and although it was approaching midwinter in the southern hemisphere, he was determined to set sail again very soon. If the stay at Dusky Sound was taken into account, then both the crews had already enjoyed several weeks of leisure and Cook considered that this was sufficient for them. He estimated that by sailing in a latitude of 45° the conditions at sea would be no worse than a winter crossing of the Atlantic. The ships were accordingly made ready for sea and on 7 June they set sail through the Cook Straits to the Pacific.

The weather was rough with high winds and rain: there was some fog but no ice or snow to contend with. The little convoy headed eastwards into uncharted waters – they were sailing about 5° south of the westward track of *Endeavour* and they held the course for about six weeks. It was an uneventful journey and there was not a speck of land to be seen. On 17 July they headed thankfully northwards towards the tropics to pick up the trade winds and warmer weather. The ships managed to keep together without too much trouble, but on 23 July the *Adventure* reported a problem. The cook, Murdoch Mahoney, died. The cause of his death was scurvy. He was not greatly mourned since he was an indolent man who never washed himself and obviously paid no attention to Cook's instructions on the ship's diet. Cook must have been very annoyed by this state of affairs, particularly with Furneaux, who was responsible for implementing his instructions on the diet of his crew. Unfortunately, the disease was not confined to the cook; many others on board the *Adventure* were also suffering from scurvy. In fact, a time came when the suffering was so bad that men from the *Resolution* had to be transferred across to work the stricken ship.

By 3 August, the ships were in the tropics and they continued north to the latitude of Tahiti before heading westwards. Tahiti would provide the fresh fruit and vegetables needed to cure the disease. The approach was planned at about 1° north of the *Endeavour*'s track in the hope that new islands would be discovered. Land was soon sighted, but it was not a new discovery. The ships passed the island of Tauere, first seen by Bougainville, and then the island of Tekokota, which they called Doubtful Island. Discounting the landing in Tasmania, this tiny speck of land was the first new discovery of the voyage after eighteen long months at sea. As they came nearer, the approaches to Tahiti were familiar to those who had been there before. Cook knew all about the dangerous coral reefs and he left orders to steer a course well clear of them, but the nightwatch ignored his instructions, or perhaps they fell asleep. Whatever the reason, when day broke, they found themselves within half a league of a dangerous reef. The Tahitians had sighted the ships and they were soon surrounding them, shouting excitedly and trying to trade. The more forward of the Tahitian girls were soon aboard the ship, negotiating a reward for their sexual favours. The girls were premature. Both the *Resolution* and the *Adventure* were in great danger. The current was carrying them rapidly towards the sharp coral of the reef. There was no wind and the sea was too deep for the anchors to claw a hold on the bottom. The warping machines, which could haul a ship into harbour, were of no avail at a place where they had no fixture ashore or under the water to anchor on to. Cook described the danger in his journal. At one point, the *Resolution* was actually striking against the coral with every swell of the sea:

About 2 o'Clock in the PM we came before an opening in the reef by which I hoped to enter with the Sloops as our situation became more and more dangerous, but when I examined the natives about it they told me that the Water was not deep and this I found upon examination, it however caused such an indraught of the Tide as was very near proving fatal to both the Sloops, the Resolution especially, for as soon as the Sloops came into this indraught they were carried by it toward the reef at a great rate; the moment I perceived this I order'd one of the Warping Machines which we had in readiness to be carrid out with about 3 or 4 hundred fathoms of rope to it, this proved of no service to us, it even would not bring her head to Sea. We then let go an anchor as soon as we could find bottom but by such time as the Ship was brought up she was in less then 3 fathom water and Struck at every fall of the Sea which broke with great violence against the reef close under our stern and threatened us every moment with ship-wreck, the Adventure anchored close to us on our starboard bow and happily did not touch. We presently carried out a Kedge Anchor and a hawser and the Coasting Anchor with an 8 inch Hawser bent to it, by heaving upon these and cuting away the Bower Anchor we saved the Ship; by the time this was done the currant or Tide had ceased to act in the same direction and then I order'd all the Boats to try to tow off the Resolution, as soon as I saw it was practical we hove up the two small anchors. At that moment a very light air came of from the land which with the assistance of the Boats by 7 o'Clock gave us an offing of about 2 Miles and I sent all the Boats to the assistance of the *Adventure*, but before they reached her she had got under sail with the land wind, leaving behind her three anchors, her coasting Cable and two Hawsers which were never recovered: thus the Sloops were got once more into safety after a narrow escape of being Wrecked on the very Island we but a few days ago so ardently wished to be at.[2]

Anders Sparrman was not a seaman, but the danger was very obvious to him. He was impressed with the way the seamen worked together to handle the crisis, but he was not amused by the bad language which came out – not only from the sailors, but also from the officers and the captain. He describes a very unusual event, when James Cook lost his cool and panicked at the danger the ships had got themselves into:

It is impossible to give a true rendering of our perilous position. None but a seaman can realise how terrible was the sound of the waves breaking on the coral reef so near to us, mingled with the shouting of orders and the noise of the operations our dangerous position necessitated. Even in my anxiety, however, I drew no small satisfaction from remarking the celerity and the lack of confusion with which each command was executed to save the ship. No one seemed aware that he had worked for more than one and a half hours under a burning sun with the thermometer at 90° in the shade.

I should have preferred, however, to hear fewer 'Goddamns' from the officers and particularly the Captain, who, while the danger lasted, stamped about the deck and grew hoarse with shouting. I have sailed with captains capable of imposing the most perfect obedience and the most delicate manoeuvres without swearing, and I am convinced that under the circumstances in which we found ourselves the same results could have been achieved with fewer oaths.[3]

The incident had clearly been a great strain on Cook. Both Forster and Sparrman described him as being in a great sweat. Although the ship had actually struck the reef, it was shaken but not badly damaged. Once the danger was over, the ships made for the safe harbour of Matavia Bay and the reunion with the Tahitians could be properly addressed. The situation quickly became far more relaxed and on an entirely different note George Forster, through eyes which were seeing Tahiti for the first time, poetically described it as the paradise of the Pacific:

It was one of those beautiful mornings which the poets of all nations have attempted to describe, when we saw the isle of Otaheite, within two miles before us. The east-wind, which had carried us so far, was entirely vanished, and a faint breeze only wafted a delicious perfume from the land, and curled the surface of the sea. The mountains, clothed with forests, rose majestic in various spiry forms, on which we already perceived the light of the rising sun; nearer to the eye a lower range of hills, easier of ascent, appeared, wooded like the former, and coloured with several pleasing hues of green, soberly mixed with autumnal browns. At their foot lay the plain, crowned with its fertile bread-fruit trees, over which rose innumerable palms, the princes of the grove. Here everything seemed as yet asleep, the morning scarce dawned, and a peaceful shade still rested on the landscape. We discerned, however, a number of houses among the trees, and many canoes hauled up along the sandy beaches. About half a mile from the shore a ledge of rocks level with the water, extended parallel to the land, on which the surf broke, leaving a smooth and secure harbour within. The sun beginning to illuminate the plain, its inhabitants arose and enlivened the scene. Having perceived the large vessels on their coast, several of them hastened to the beach, launched their canoes, and paddled towards us.[4]

The people of Tahiti had changed very little in the four years that had passed since Cook had been there with the *Endeavour*. Excited chattering islanders surrounded the ship in their canoes – they were willing to trade fruit, vegetables and poultry in exchange for nails and other small items from the ship. They had not changed in their pilfering habits and Cook had to fire a musket over the head of one of the thieves to scare him away. When this did not have the desired effect on the rest of the gathering, he fired a four-pounder from the ship's cannon. This frightened the Tahitians so much that some of them scurried off to the hills. They quickly returned to satisfy their curiosity, but Cook noticed that the guns had frightened a small boy in one of the canoes. Here we get another glimpse of Cook's character: he went out of his way to seek out the boy and gave him some beads to overcome his fright.

The *Resolution* and the *Adventure* were not so much of a novelty in

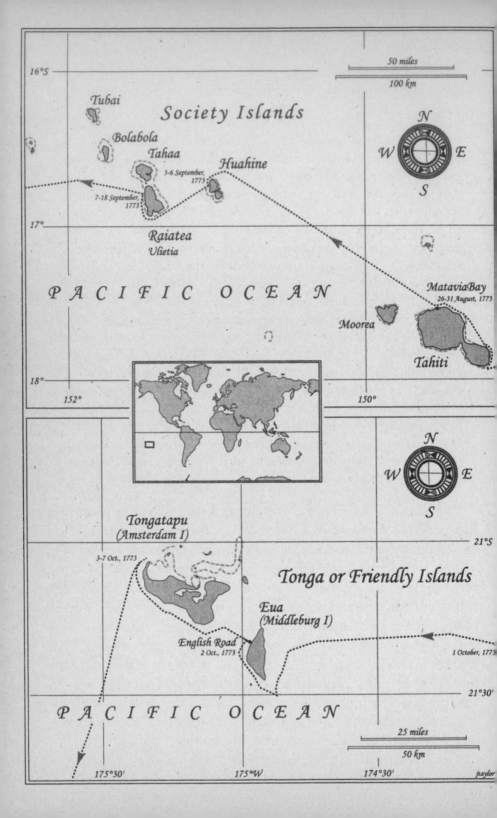

Tahiti as the earlier European vessels had been. Both the French and the Spanish had anchored there since Cook's last visit and this was one of the reasons why the island's hogs, an excellent supply of fresh meat, were not as plentiful as Cook had hoped. Another problem was that of the island politics. These were so volatile that the Tahitians seemed to manage a bloodless revolution every two years. The chief of the island was a very young man, a youth of about eighteen, called Ereti, O'Rette or Otou – different accounts cannot agree on the spelling of his name. Cook remembered Otou from 1769 as a youth of about fourteen. He was the son of an old man with a white beard called Vehiatua. The son was now firmly established as the Aree, or king, of Tahiti. Otou had fine flaxen hair, regular features and a dark olive complexion. He sat on a high stool with his courtiers, who were stripped to the waist when attending him. He wore no more than a white sash round his middle, with his upper body and his legs uncovered. Otou was ruler of the island, but Forster got the impression that he was very timorous, afraid of the newcomers and also nervous about some of his own subjects. For Richard Pickersgill, who was on his third visit to Tahiti, Otou was the third leader he had encountered in five years. He wanted to track down Queen Oberea, also known as Purea, the happy ruler of the island on his first visit with Captain Wallis in the *Dolphin*. He did manage to find his queen eventually, but only with great difficulty, and he found that she was in badly reduced circumstances. The former queen of Tahiti was living in such poverty that she was unable to supply as much as an island hog for the ships' supplies.

The religion on Tahiti was as difficult to understand as the politics. Forster conducted a close examination of the marae, which he knew were memorials to the dead. He was able to obtain Tahitian clothing and dressed himself like the natives – a gesture that they seemed to appreciate. At one of the marae, he found a shrine and the corpse of a woman who had recently died. She was elevated on a platform about breast high: there was an altar and a priest or keeper in attendance. The keeper allowed him to take the coconuts and bananas which seemed to be left as offerings to the dead or to the gods. At one place he discovered fifteen long pieces of wood carved with fantastic Tahitian figures, male and female, promiscuously entwined around each other with the males positioned above the females.

The Tahitians had lost nothing of their hospitality and entertained the visitors with a play, a comedy acted out by five men and one woman, the sister to Otoú. The entertainment lasted about an hour and a half. There was some musical accompaniment on the drums, but the British could not follow the plot that was delivered in the Tahitian language. The hospitality extended to plenty of contact with the Tahitian women, but the journals do not make as much of the sexual contact as on the previous voyages. William Wales gives a detached description of the Tahitian women. He begins with an apology for what may be interpreted as his lack of taste:

> With regard to the Personal Beauties of the Otahitean Ladies, I believe it would be most prudent to remain entirely silent; since by a contrary preceedure I must expose in the grossest manner my own want of tast, or that of those Gentlemen who have asserted that 'they may vie with the greatest beauties of Europe', and that 'the English Women appeared Verry ordinery on their first arrival there' from this celebrated Cythera: but it is no new thing for the itch of writing to get the better of prudence; it will not therefore be wondered at if I run all risks of this kind to have the pleasure of describing their persons; at least, so far as there appears to be any national characteristic in it. In the first place then their stature is very small, and their features although rather regular have a masculine turn. Their Complexion is a light Olive, or rather a deadish Yellow; their hair is of a glossy black and cut short in the bowl-dish fashion of the Country People in England; but had here, I think, a pretty effect, as it corresponded more with the simplicity of their Dress than any other form would. Their Eyes are exceeding black and lively but rather too prominent for my liking. Their noses are flat especially towards the lower end and their nostrils in consequence wide, as are also their mouths. Their lips are rather thick than otherwise: but their teeth are remarkable close, white, and even.[5]

The welcome supply of fresh fruit and vegetables helped the crew of the *Adventure* to make a rapid recovery from scurvy, and when the men were fit enough to sail, Cook was anxious to be on his way. He did not wish to outstay his welcome and on 3 September he set sail for the islands of Huahine and Raiatea, which he knew were only one or two days' sail to the north-west. The journey was uneventful, except for the final approach to Huahine, where there was a repeat of the situation at Tahiti. Cook got his ship safely inside the reef but the *Adventure* timed the approach badly and was in danger of striking against the coral. This time, Cook was well prepared for the danger. He already had a boat in the water to give assistance to the other ship and the situation was quickly recovered. They landed to the usual friendly reception from the indigenous population. Pickersgill was immediately despatched to find a supply of hogs and Cook set out with Forster and Furneaux to try and find Oree, the king of the island whom he had last seen about four years ago. It did not take the captain long to find his friend: William Wales described Oree as an elderly, thin and grave man much revered by his subjects. Oree was not afraid to show his emotions and his reunion with Captain Cook was a tearful and moving affair. No doubt they never expected that they would ever meet again when they lived on opposite sides of the world. Cook described his reception:

> After they had done sending the things above mentioned to the Boat, our guide who still remained in the boat with us desired to decorate three young Plantain plants with Nails, looking glasses Medals etc etc, which was accordingly done, we landed with These in our hands and walked up towards the Chief a lane being made by the people between us and him for here were a vast crowd. We were made to sit down before we came to the chief, our Plantains were then taken from us one by one and laid down by him, one was for Eatoua or God, the Second for the Arree or King and the third for Tyo or friendship. This being done Oree rose up came and fell upon my neck and embraced me, this was by no means ceremonious the tears which trinckled plentifully down his Cheeks sufficiently spoke the feelings of his heart. All his friends were next interduced to us among whome was a beautifull Boy his grandson. The whole ceremony being now over I made him the present I had prepared consisting of the most Valuable articles I had for this purpose and in return he gave me a Hog and a quantity of Cloth and promised that all our wants should be supplied and it will soon appear how well he kept his word, at length we took leave and return'd aboard to dinner and some time after the Cutter arrived with 14 Hogs, many more were purchased on shore and a long side the Sloops.[6]

The reception was marred by an unfortunate incident involving the Swedish botanist Anders Sparrman. He went off on his own to collect

botanical specimens but, unknown to him, he had been followed by
two local men. They attacked him and stole his sword and clothing,
including the shirt from his back. According to some accounts, poor
Sparrman was forced to return to the ship naked, but it seems from
Cook's journal that he was at least allowed to keep his trousers on. It
was certainly the worst case of theft on the whole voyage. Sparrman
describes the details of the incident in his own words:

> My two friends soon turned out to be knaves, for no sooner were we
> some miles on our way, and out of sight of the native dwellings, than
> they threw themselves upon me, reiterating that I was their *tayo maitai*,
> or good friend. One of them at once tore off my hunting knife and the
> belt I wore round my waist. Hardly had I freed my throat from the grip
> of the other, who had almost strangled me, before I received a blow on
> the head with my own knife which made me see stars, and felled me to
> the ground, where I lay upon my side. The two brigands took advantage
> of my plight and buried themselves upon me as soon as I tried to rise to
> my feet. They seized me by the coat, which split right down the back
> while I was doing my best to deal them blows in the belly. I sought for
> stones, but found none. However, I feigned to have found some and made
> movements as if to throw them, whereupon they withdrew and I made
> my way to the beach. But when they saw that I had nothing in my hands
> they pursued me with the drawn knife.

Anders Sparrman tried to run away from them. He seemed to have
succeeded, but then he found that he was lost and didn't know the way
back to the ship. His flight was impeded by the thick growth of what
he identified as *Convolvuli brasilienses* underfoot. He was forced to change
tactics and stopped dead. The man with the knife gave him a few light
blows about the head and shoulders. The second thief succeeded in
grabbing the botanist by the shirt and tried to pull it over his head. As
the shirt was securely buttoned at the wrist, the man was unable to
get it off. At first, Sparrman took it very calmly. He thought the
situation seemed somewhat comical until he realised that the brigand
with the knife was quite capable of slashing his arms to obtain the
shirt. He tried addressing him in a friendly fashion and said: '*Area tayo
eaha te matte*' – that is to say, 'Wait, my friend, and do not kill me.' He
unbuttoned the wristband with his left hand and then did the same
with his right. Once free of his shirt, he countered the attacker holding

the knife, getting close up under his right arm so that he could not stab with it. The other Huahinean ran off with his booty, quickly followed by his partner in crime, who had been trying to tear off poor Sparrman's trousers. The botanist hastened to regain the track back to the ship. He armed himself with some stones, one in each fist. When he came within reach of the other islanders, he found that they were willing to help him:

> Meanwhile the villains were encouraging each other to renew the attack, but they recoiled when they perceived the stones I carried and, shortly afterwards, I reached some native houses. The people were greatly alarmed to see me thus, half naked and bleeding, and no doubt thought that I was about to revenge myself upon them for the wrongs inflicted upon me, so they all fled crying and wailing, except a young man and an old one, both of whom seemed exceedingly touched by my plight. The old man took off a cloak and covered my bare shoulders with it. They themselves were much afraid that the bandits would return.
>
> When, finally, red with anger and out of breath, I reached the market I saw many of my friends turn pale at the sight of me. I gave them to understand that my adventure must be regarded as an abominable insult, albeit feeling no pain from the injuries I had received. The only serious loss I had sustained, and one which I much regretted, was that of my microscope, and the greatest discomfort I endured was from the loss of one shoe, the upper leather of which had come off during the fight with my assailants.

It was a serious breach of trust by the Huahineans. An official complaint was made to King Oree and he was very upset about this breach of hospitality by his people. The thieves had fled into the mountains and it would take time to track them down, but the island was not large and, with the help of the chief and his sister, the sword and a part of Sparmann's waistcoat were brought back. The garment had been cut into pieces — the remaining part of his waistcoat was promised for the next day.

There was one thing that remained unchanged from Cook's previous visit. This was the perennial war with the Bolabola men which was still in force. In fact, the Bolabola men controlled all the islands in the local group except Huahine. Oree wanted Cook to help him with the dispute and to use the ship's great guns against his enemies, but Cook

would have nothing to do with local politics. He knew from his previous
visit that the feared Bolabola men would be friendly towards him if he
treated them with the proper respect. Cook chose not to visit Bolabola,
but in spite of entreaties from the chief he sailed for neighbouring
island of Raiatea (or Ulieteah) which was under Bolabola control. At
Raiatea, he met two chiefs from Bolabola. One was called Oruherra.
He was tattooed all over his chest, belly and back with broad bands
and a pattern of squares: his hands and thighs were quite black with
tattoos. The other chief was called Hiria and he was the largest person
they had seen in the Pacific. He measured 44 inches around the waist
and $31\frac{3}{4}$ inches around his thighs. His hair was arranged in thick tufts.

Cook's reception at Raiatea was almost as emotional as at Huahine.
The high regard in which the Society Islands held James Cook is a great
testimony to his respectful and considerate handling of the people. The
name of the chief, Oreo, was almost identical to Oree at Huahine, which
leads us to suspect that the name meant 'king' or 'chieftain'. The king
of the neighbouring island of Otaha was called Otah after the island. A
great crowd of islanders thronged around to see the newcomers. The
Raiateans put on an impromptu entertainment consisting of music and
dancing with three drums, seven male dancers and one female. William
Wales described the drums in detail. They gave out different tones.
The smallest was twelve to fourteen inches deep and about the same
in diameter, the middle drum about thirty inches deep and ten in
diameter, the longest drum about forty-two inches deep with a diameter of seven or eight inches. The membranes were of shark's skin kept
taut by a bracing arrangement similar to the European system, and the
drums were beaten with the fingers. The female dancer was young girl
of about fifteen. Her name was Poetua and she was the daughter of the
chief. She was of middling stature, slender with regular features, and
she had dark hair, fine white teeth and flashing bright eyes in her dusky
face. She was a talented and very popular dancer. She took a liking to
Richard Pickersgill and invited him into her dressing-room. He
recorded the incident in some detail:

> After we had been in this House a little while Miss Poedoua [Poetua] for
> that was her name, desired me to go and see her Dress: we went to an
> ajacent House, the front of which was open and opposite it at the
> distance of about ten yards between these two Houses was a space neatly

cover'd with Matts, on these Matts they acted. In the first House sat the audience and in the Second the Musick, one end being inclosed for the actresses to dress in, which was in closed: into this Place she carried me, where undressing an old woman came in to dress her; her Dress consisted of large Pieces of Painted Cloths made up in folds and girded tort round her to an amazing thickness, and her head dressed in the Manner of a Turband with fine Platted black hair ornimented with flowers.[9]

The evening's entertainment ended with a dance and comedy from the younger men. It seemed to be a burlesque parody ridiculing the chiefs of the island. There were four drums and some boy singers. The male dancing was admired, but their gestures and facial expressions seemed ludicrous though amusing to the Europeans. The man who seemed to enjoy and understand the plot more then the others was James Burney. He tells us that one man was so expressive that he was likened to the famous Drury Lane actor David Garrick:

At Ulietea I saw one of their Heava's or dances. I shall only say of their dancing that in 5 minutes time they commonly go through all their manoeuvres – the rest is a continual repetition – but what afforded me much more entertainment, was at every interval between their dancing, small dramatic pieces were acted by way of interludes to intertain the Spectators while the dancers took breath. These were performd by men – they have a great deal of good action, one in particular whom we nicknamd Garrick expressed the passions so lively in his looks, Voice & actions that we easily dived into his meaning & understood the plots of most of their pieces – Every now and then the Spectators would break into immoderate fits of laughter at some jest which was lost to us from our little knowledge of their language – however we were able to comprehend the story – I will give you a small account of one.
    The Master of a family before Night puts every thing in its proper place & sees all in order – after which the whole family go to sleep presently in comes the Thief who conveys every thing he lays hold of to his Companions who wait without – after playing many dextrous tricks one of the family wakes & alarms the rest – they all get up & grope about the Thief (you are to supose it quite dark) & one of them gets hold of his Cloaths which the Thief immediately slips off, puts over a post & makes his escape – the other all this time holds fast & calls for a light, thinking he had caught the Rogue – the light comes & he is

undeceivd – & finds every thing moveable carried off – The Master falls in a passion, beats his Servants for their Carelessness they promise to behave better & the piece concludes –

This, you'll say, is not poetical justice, unless they account Negligence a greater crime than dishonesty.[10]

It was well known that the Frenchman Bougainville had taken a South Sea islander back on his ship to France and to Parisian society. The British were keen to emulate the French and there was no shortage of volunteers from the Society Islands to make the journey. There was much discussion about the ethics of taking an innocent Polynesian islander back to England and to the very different kind of life they could expect there. Cook himself was against the idea, but he bowed to the pressure of the other members of the expedition. Thus, when he was at Tahiti, Cook had taken on a man called Porio in the hope that he would be a useful interpreter at the other islands he planned to visit, but Porio only lasted a few days. He took a great liking to one of the girls from the island of Raiatea and decided to leave the ship in favour of his lady friend. Cook could hardly object to this love match and replaced his Tahitian readily enough with Odiddy, a native of the island of Bolabola. Odiddy was keen to sail for distant lands. He soon proved himself to be a promising and useful addition to the expedition, but Cook realised that he was not as good a communicator as his old friend Tupia on the *Endeavour* voyage. Furneaux also took on board one of the local men. His name was Omai, a native of Huahine. It transpired that Omai was the only one of these three Polynesians to see England.

The visit to the Society Islands was necessary for the restocking of the ship and it was also a social call for renewing old acquaintances, but the main reason for this part of the voyage was to try and locate the islands seen by the explorers of old and to establish their latitude and longitude. On 18 September the two ships left the Society Islands to sail to the west in search of a landfall made by Abel Tasman in what became known as the Tonga Isles. The extent of Tasman's voyage of 1642–3 was amazing in that he made four major discoveries, namely Tasmania, New Zealand, the Tonga islands and the Fijian islands. He also circumnavigated Australia, although he saw hardly anything of the coastline. His voyage lasted less than a year, and he did not sail from Holland but from the Dutch East Indies. It was an incredible 130 years before the places found by Tasman were rediscovered. Some of the outlying islands in the Tonga group had been sighted but had never been revisited. Cook knew that Tasman's account was sufficiently accurate to be worth following up and he knew that by running down the right latitude he stood an excellent chance of rediscovering the islands.

After five days' sailing to the west, a small, isolated and uninhabited island was sighted, which Cook named Sandwich Island. Alexander Dalrymple, according to his book, thought the island had been sighted in the early seventeenth century by Quiros, but this was no more than guesswork. The *Resolution* and the *Adventure* sailed westwards, following the setting sun for another eight days and then, on 1 October, an island was sighted ahead. Cook felt confident from the latitude that they were approaching the islands that Tasman had called Middleburg and Amsterdam. He was soon able to establish that the local names were Eua and Tongatapu.

An immense crowd came out in their canoes and swarmed around the ships to greet them and, when they were closer, some came swimming out from the shore to join in the reception. The islanders were excited, chattering, curious and friendly. They had no fear or hostility, and there were no weapons to be seen, not even a stick. The ships worked their way through the flotilla of canoes to the west coast, where they found a suitable anchorage. Cook was able to identify the harbour as the one used by Tasman.

It is easy to see why the unannounced arrival of two ships such as the *Resolution* and the *Adventure* – modest ships by European standards but huge, tall and exciting to South Sea islanders – caused such excitement when they were seen for the first time. The hairy, red-faced, fair-skinned sailors in their unfamiliar clothing and the elaborate uniforms of the officers, the contents and the strange artefacts of the ship, the huge swelling sails and the tangle of ropes and rigging – all these were things of great wonder to the Tongans. As with all the islands visited by the early explorers, there was always a missing factor. The people of the Pacific Islands had their oral traditions, but they did not have a written record. What were the feelings and emotions of the Tongans when they saw the two strange vessels approaching their islands? Was there any memory of a similar incident from many years ago? Was there anything surviving in their folklore, handed down over five or six generations? Even if the tradition had survived, it would have been a very garbled version of contact with an unknown outside world, which was very alien to those who lived and died in their island community. From their birth, these were a people who never expected to find more in the world than that contained in their scattered Pacific Islands.

In many respects, the Tonga islands were very similar to the Society Islands. The trade, the vegetables and the supplies were similar. The same friendly greeting of rubbing noses was practised. Some dyed their hair in shades of red and blue, some were tattooed in a fashion reminiscent of Tahiti and many had mutilated the end of their little finger, which was a mark of respect for a lost relative. The unfortunate trait of thieving was just as bad here as on the other islands. The worst incident occurred when a man sneaked into the captain's cabin and was spotted escaping with an armful of rulers, navigational instruments and a copy of the *Nautical Almanac* – none of which were of any possible use to him, but he simply coveted the ownership of such rare and alien artefacts. The astronomer had his shoes stolen from under his nose and was marooned in his bare feet on the sharp coral. Luckily, the captain was able to recover the footwear quickly for him.

There were some subtle differences between the Society Islands and the Tongas. Firstly there was the language. It was different from the Society Islands but the difference seemed to be no more than a local variation or dialect. There were minor differences in the flora and fauna, and one of the main items of trade, which became of great value later in the voyage, was the bright red feathers of the tropical birds. One of the main reasons for taking Odiddy and Omai on the expedition was to help with communication. Both of them must have been good at picking up English or Cook would not have accepted them so readily, but to the captain's dismay neither of them could understand the Tongan dialect. The politics and religion were, as usual, very confusing. Cook had great problems trying to locate the head man of the island, and when he eventually found a very elderly man who was treated with great respect as the islanders' leader, he found that he could make no communication at all with him. The man took so little notice of Cook that both he and Forster came to the conclusion that he was an idiot. They may have come to the correct conclusion, but it seemed to be a tradition that the king did not speak with anybody and that he acknowledged nothing – it was all very puzzling to the European mind.

There were, however, a great many good points that put the Tongans culturally above any people previously discovered in the Pacific. When it came to the evening entertainment, Cook ordered music from the ship's bagpipes. The Tongans followed with a musical concert where three young women sang and danced. The Tongan music came as a very pleasant surprise. The monotonous music of Tahiti consisted of only three notes, the Maoris had advanced their musical scale to five notes, but in the Tonga Isles they had the full range of harmony. Flutes were made of bamboo with four to six pipes and they were blown using the nostril. There were other instruments with ten or eleven reed pipes that could play a note on each pipe. Drums were made from hollow logs and were beaten with hardwood sticks. The dancing girls were beautiful, clear-skinned and bare-breasted as they danced to the flutes and drums. The girls beat the time in unison. They snapped their first fingers against their thumbs and moving together, held their other three fingers aloft. Cook presented them with a necklace each. The performance certainly appealed to James Burney, the son of the famous musician Dr Charles Burney. He was sufficiently impressed to take down and record the tune, which proved of great interest in the Burney household when he returned to England.

The Tongan canoes, with platforms, sails and outriggers, were superior in construction to any they had seen before. They were neat and robust, cleverly made by sewing wooden slats together with a cord made from coconut fibre. The sewing was executed so that no stitching was visible on the outside. Houses were round or oval-shaped, very basic but well constructed and containing wickerwork furniture and partitions. The island was beautifully laid out with plantations in neat rows. They grew coconuts, breadfruit, plantains or bananas, lemons, yams, a kind of apple, sugar cane and root crops. The islanders built very neat and strong boundary fences separating one man's private property from that of his neighbour. Green roads separated the plantations, and shrines to commemorate the dead were located at some of the crossroads. Cook looked at one of the shrines and gave a detailed description of the area:

After we had [d]one examining this place of worship which in their Language is called Afia-tou-ca we desired to return, but instead of conducting us directly to the Water side they struck into a road leading into the Country, this road which was a very publick one, was about [16] feet broad and as even as a B[owling] green, there was a fence of reeds on each side and here and there doors which opened into the adjoining Plantations; several other Roads from different parts joined this, some equally as broad and others narrower, the most part of them shaded from the Scorching Sun by fruit trees. I thought I was transported into one of the most fertile plains in Europe, here was not an inch of waste ground, the roads occupied no more space than was absolutely necessary and each fence did not take up above 4 Inches and even this was not wholy lost for in many of the fences were planted fruit trees and the Cloth plant, these served as a support to them, it was every were the same, change of place altered not the sene. Nature, assisted by a little art, no were appears in a more florishing state than at this isle. In these delightfull Walks we met numbers of people some were traveling down to the Ships with their burdthens of fruit, others returning back empty, they all gave us the road and either sit down or stood up with their backs against the fences till we had pass'd . . ."

The only problem was the supply of water, which almost everywhere turned out to be brackish. The islanders got over this problem by drinking coconut milk, but to Cook and his men this was no substitute for pure water. Luckily, there was one solitary supply of fresh water which Cook identified as the same source used by Tasman on his visit long ago.

A man called Atago visited every morning. He proved to be very helpful and Cook rewarded him with the gift of a dog and a bitch, for there seemed to be no dog population on the islands. The Tongans dressed in a single piece of cloth wrapped around the waist and both sexes were naked above. On their arms and necks they wore simple ornaments of shells, beads and mother of pearl. The people were seen as neither ugly nor attractive, but for all his faults the elder Forster had a keen eye for beauty in all cultures. He picked out a young girl from the crowd whom he felt sure would be a beauty in any society:

There was in the Crowd a young Girl with the most regular features & the sweetest Countenance, her Eye was bright & lively & was all Soul:

her long black hair hung negligently down: all her Limbs were proportion & Symmetry. Her actions easy and brisk. She had five apples &
threw them continually up in the Air & caught them with an amazing
activity and skill. She was very young, not above 10 or 12 years old: &
may it not displease our northern fair ones, I believe, if properly edu-
cated & dressed she would have shone in the most brilliant Circles of
Brittish Beauties, & caused emulation among her sex & admiration in
the other.[12]

The existence of the islands had been confirmed and their longitude
had been measured to within half a degree. The Tongans were able to
navigate short distances by using the stars, and they traded with
other islands to the north – these were smaller islands than Eua and
Tongatapu but there were many of them. Cook had no time to investigate further, however. It was October and spring was well advanced
in the southern hemisphere. The summer months were approaching,
and he had to make full use of them to explore the high latitudes. It
was time to sail again for New Zealand to make his preparations. The
tropical interlude had been an immense success: the Antarctic seemed
an infinite distance away and the men were happy and relaxed. Cook
paid the Tongans the great compliment of calling their group the
Friendly Isles. Lieutenant Clerke, who had sailed with Cook on the
Endeavour, summarised the findings in the Society Islands and the
Friendly Isles:

I must own that 'tis with some reluctance, that I bid adieu to these
happy Isles, where I've spent many very happy days, both in the years
69 & 73; in the first place (for we must give this consideration the
preference after a long Sea passage) you live upon, and abound in, the
very best Pork and the sweetest and most salutary of Vegetables; in the
next place, the Women in general are very handsome and very kind, and
the Men civil and to the last degree benevolent, so that I'm sure when-
ever we get among them we may with very great safety say, We've got
into a very good Neighbourhood – in short, in my Opinion, they are as
pleasant & Happy spots as this World contains.

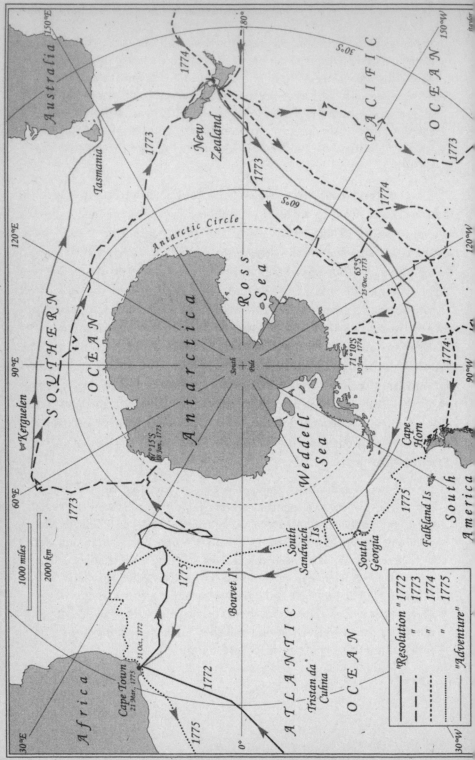

SIX

To the Ends of the Earth

*After that our ships reached the deep sea; no longer could any
land be seen – just sea and sky on every side.*

Aeneid, III, 192

The Tongan island group lies a little to the east of New Zealand and
Cook knew that the shortest route was a course almost due south
which would take him past the north cape and on to the east coast of
the North Island. He knew from his previous voyage that the Maoris
on the east coast were more involved with cultivation and generally
more advanced than the residents of Queen Charlotte Sound. The
passage took about two weeks, with the *Adventure* once again trailing
behind her sister ship. On 21 October a great black cloud covered the
sky – the ships had to fire their guns to keep together – but on the
next day the weather improved and land was sighted when Table Cape
was identified about nine leagues to the west. After another day's sail,
the ships were at Cape Kidnappers, where they were able to make
contact and trade with the Maoris who remembered Cook from his
first visit. The captain was determined to do as much as possible to
advance the New Zealand economy. He left pigs and fowl with them,
seeds and root vegetables, and also a large spike nail that the local chief
greatly appreciated.

He set sail along the coast, but the next day the gales started in
earnest. The *Resolution*'s top gallant was taken away by the storm and
James Cook found it impossible to get into the straits which were
named after him. Four years previously, he had sailed through the Cook
Straits from the opposite direction. He knew that they were difficult
waters, but he had not reckoned with the New Zealand weather. The

storm was so ferocious that Cook had no option but to ride it out with
every mast bare of canvas. The *Adventure* was lost but she was found
again. The ships were carried out to sea about nine leagues south-east
of Cape Palliser. For several days, the bad weather prevented either
ship from entering Cook Strait. Then the ships parted company for a
second time. Sparrman recounted:

> Now the storm increased to such an extent that on Monday morning,
> the 25th of October, we were compelled to heave to with a single sail;
> fortunately the wind blew from the shore, for had it come with similar
> strength and driven us towards instead of from the land, neither ship
> would have had any hope of salvation. Although we were in the lee of
> the high land, we were not adequately protected from wind and seas,
> but were dashed about most grievously. We saw the spray and foam
> raised by the wind and driven in steaming drops like drifting snow in
> the severest storm, so that the whole surface of the sea seemed covered
> with clouds; nevertheless, clear sunbeams frequently penetrated the
> mist, and shimmered and broke against the seething crests of the waves,
> so that our eyes were dazzled. The force of the gale soon tore to shreds
> the only sail we had dared to hoist, and the ship made her way under
> bare poles; sometimes she listed so that green seas rushed in with a
> weight and power that destroyed and swept away everything in their
> course.[1]

At last, on 1 November, the *Resolution* rounded Cape Campbell and
entered the straits that separated the North and South Islands, but as
she did so the gale rose up again from the north-west. Cook ran his
ship into Cloudy Bay, looking for shelter. It was here that he missed
the opportunity of exploring the harbours to the north of the straits
and charting what became Wellington Harbour. He was too busy and
anxious to make the rendezvous with the *Adventure* at Ship Cove. It
was here also that the young George Forster wrote a few prophetic
words about this part of New Zealand:

> Perhaps in future ages, when the maritime powers of Europe lose their
> American colonies, they may think of making new establishments in
> more distant regions: and if it were ever possible for Europeans to have
> humanity enough to acknowledge the indigenous tribes of the South
> Sea as their brethren, we might have settlements which would not be
> defiled by the blood of innocent nations.[2]

It was two more days before the *Resolution* made her way out again from Cloudy Bay into the Cook Straits. It had taken so long to get through that Cook was confident of finding his sister ship already anchored there. He placed too much confidence in Furneaux, however, and for this second rendezvous the *Adventure* was not waiting there to greet him. It was frustrating to lose company a second time but it did not seem a major calamity. There was much to do to prepare the ship for the next leg of the voyage and the *Adventure* would surely turn up during the weeks of preparation. Cook was planning to undertake a long voyage to the coldest climes on the planet. He was to sail again for the Antarctic – this time in the longitudes of the southern Pacific.

The provisioning went well enough, with up to 150 canoes gathering round to trade, but the Maoris at Queen Charlotte Sound were a disappointment: they had killed and eaten the goats and fowl that had been left behind. Furneaux's vegetable garden had been left untended, but all the same it had managed to produce a small crop to help out with the provisioning. It seemed that the hog and the sow had managed to survive without any human intervention. There was an incident on 23 November when Pickersgill discovered the head and body of a recently killed youth. There had been much discussion about whether or not the Maoris were cannibals and there was only one way to prove it beyond all doubt. The head was brought back to the ship and part of the flesh was cut off and roasted. One of the Maoris ate it with great relish in front of all those present. Never before had the British witnessed the gruesome act of eating human flesh. The crew were dismayed and disgusted. The Tahitian Odiddy was even more revolted than the British, but the Maoris simply laughed at his discomfort. Wales noted Odiddy's discomfort:

> Terror took possession of him the moment he saw the piece of meat cut off, and the Man eat it, he became perfectly motionless, and seemed as if Metamorphosed into the Statue of Horror: it is, I believe, utterly impossible for Art to depict that passion with half the force that it appeared in his Countenance. He continued in this situation untill some of us roused him out of it by talking to him, and then burst into Tears nor could refrain himself the whole Evening afterwards.[3]

There was much talk of cannibalism amongst officers and crew, but it was time to weigh anchor. Where was Tobias Furneaux and where was the *Adventure*? Surely he must have made it into the Cook Straits by this time? The only conclusion Cook could draw was that Furneaux had either sailed directly for Cape Horn or, perish the thought, he was shipwrecked on an unknown shore of New Zealand. But the Antarctic voyage could wait no longer. The seasons were moving on and it was imperative to make the most of the southern summer. Cook decided that he must sail on his own. By the twenty-seventh he was through the straits. He made a cursory but unsuccessful search for the *Adventure* and then he set sail for the deep south.

The *Adventure* had struggled hard to keep up with the *Resolution*. After the ships had been separated by the storm, Furneaux managed to make landfall near Cape Palliser. He traded successfully with the Maoris for crayfish and other supplies. For two days the wind blew hard from the north-west and it was impossible to get around Cape Palliser. Much praise has rightly been lavished on the Whitby ships, but they were not all up to the standard of the *Endeavour* and the *Resolution*.

> Our Ship in her best trim is not able to keep up, or carry sail with the *Resolution*, at this time we fall bodily to Leeward being quite Light & so crank that we are obliged to strike to every Squall, and so unmanageable that there is no getting her round either one way or the other, on the morning of the 5th of November near Cape Palliser the wind shifted suddenly from the NW to the SSW & blew very strong – we had 3 tryals & were full $\frac{1}{4}$ of an hour before we could get her head off shore – had she failed the third time should have cut away the Mizen Mast...

The ship was in a poor state, with worn rigging and leaking decks. The leaks were so bad that the water got into the men's bedding and it was small wonder that they claimed to be very uncomfortable. The winds moved to the south-west and they sailed again past Cape Palliser, thinking they had a fair wind at last, but they were unable to make it round the cape and the wind drove them back again to the north and along the coast. In fact, Furneaux was driven right back to Tolaga Bay, where he managed to land again and to wood and water his ship. On 12 November he took to sea again, but the wind was so strong that he could not clear the headlands of the bay in either direction. He made it to sea yet again on the sixteenth and regained his position from a week before, but then it cost him a full two weeks of beating back and forth outside the straits before he had a favourable wind. Sometime during this two weeks, the *Resolution* left on her way to the Antarctic, but the ships were too far apart to see each other.

Furneaux eventually made it into Cook Straits, but it was not until 30 November that the *Adventure* limped wearily into Ship Cove and it was obvious that they had arrived too late. There was plenty of evidence that the *Resolution* had been there and Cook had gone to some pains to leave a message. At the landing place was a prominent tree with the words 'Look underneath' carved on the trunk in large letters. At the foot of the tree Cook had buried a bottle and in it was a note with his tentative sailing plans. The greeting was expressed formally in the third person:

Queen Charlotte Sound New Zealand 24 Nov 1773
    His Britannic Majesty's sloop Resolution Captain Cook arrived last in this port on the 3d instant and sailed again on the date hereof, Captain Cook intended to spend a few days in the east enterance of the straits in looking for the Adventure Captain Furneaux who he parted company with in the night of the 29th of last month, afterwards he will proceed to the South and Eastward. As Captain Cook has not the least hopes of meeting with Captain Furneaux he will not take upon him to name any place for a Rendezvous; he however thinks of retiring to Easter Island in Latd 27°6' S Longitude 108°0' West a [*sic*] Greenwich in about the latter end of next march, it is even probable that he may go to Otaheiti or the society Isles but this will depend upon so much circumstances that nothing with any degree of certainty can be depended upon.

When Omai, the Polynesian from Huahine, realised that Cook had left a message he was very impressed – so much so that he decided he must learn to read and write forthwith and pass the knowledge on to his own people in the Society Islands. James Burney and others set out to help him, but the task proved much harder than Omai had imagined. Cook's message left no specific orders for Furneaux. He was very vague about his own movements. He hadn't yet fully made up his mind about his next step beyond the Antarctic seas and he certainly hadn't

mentioned Easter Island to any of his crew. The ball was left in Furneaux's court and what he should do next was his own decision. The
location of Easter Island, as given in the message, was precise enough,
but the date of the rendezvous was no more than a rough estimate and
it would be no mean feat for the *Adventure* to find the island in the
midst of the vast Pacific. There was time for Furneaux to discuss
the plans with his lieutenants. Whatever decision was made after the
beating which the ship had taken at sea, he had to get the *Adventure*
seaworthy again for what was going to be a long voyage. Furneaux
knew that Cook's plan was to sail south and to search the high latitudes
for remnants of the great southern continent. It would be impossible
for him to find the *Resolution* in those seas and in any case his ship was
simply not up to the job. He decided to make tracks for Cape Horn,
then the Cape of Good Hope and home to England.

In the middle of December, when the *Adventure* was almost ready to
sail, the most horrific incident of the whole voyage took place. Ten
men were sent out in one of the boats to gather wild celery, but when
the evening came and darkness fell, the boat had not returned. At first
there seemed no cause for concern. It was assumed that the party had
travelled too far and had been unable to get back to the ship before
nightfall. The following morning, when the boat still failed to appear,
Furneaux very naturally became anxious about them and sent James
Burney off in a second boat with a party of marines to try to locate the
men. Burney had a good idea where the search would take them. He
enquired of the local people whether they had seen his men and he got
evasive answers. When he saw them avoiding his party and sneaking
off into the woods, he began to fear the worst. Cook and his crew
had witnessed cannibalism a few days before they left Ship Cove, but
what James Burney and his party witnessed in Grass Cove was far
worse:

> . . . the men on seeing us left their Canoe & ran up into the woods – this
> gave me reason to Suspect I should here get some tidings of our Cutter –
> we went ashore & Searchd the Canoe where we found one of the Rullock
> [rowlock] ports of the Cutter & some Shoes one of which was known to
> belong to Mr Woodhouse, one of our Midshipmen, who went with Mr
> Rowe – one of the people at the same time brought me a piece of meat,
> which he took to be some of the Salt Meat belonging to the Cutter's

Crew — on examining this & smelling to it I found it was fresh meat —
Mr Fannin, (the Master) who was with me, supos'd it was Dog's flesh &
I was of the same opinion, for I still doubted their being Cannibals: but
we were Soon convinced by most horrid & undeniable proofs — a great
many baskets (about 20) laying on the beach tied up, we cut them open,
some were full of roasted flesh & some of fern root which serves them
for bread — on further search we found more shoes & a hand which we
immediately knew to have belong'd to Thos Hill one of our Fore-
castlemen, it being markd T. H. which he had got done at Otaheite with
a tattow instrument.[6]

Burney investigated further by boat. At Grass Cove there was a
great gathering of Maoris, like a fair, with a large fire on the high land
above. The marines fired a volley to dispel them. The Maoris ignored
the first volley, but on the second they retreated and scrambled away
to the hills, except for two stout men who walked slowly and deliberately away, their pride not suffering them to run. Burney landed with
the marines. He found a broken oar stuck in the ground, but no sign of
the cutter. Then he discovered a scene of carnage and barbarity such
as he had never seen in his life. The Maoris on top of the hill were
quarrelling and making a great noise. It was growing dark and the fires
on the hill above could be seen about three miles away, spread out in a
great semicircle. He consulted with Peter Fannin. Angry as they were,
they agreed that there was no point in trying to extract revenge: it
would mean splitting the party in two, and it was beginning to rain
and he feared that the muskets would misfire.

The names of the dead were John Rowe, the master's mate; Midshipman Thomas Woodhouse; Francis Murphy, the quartermaster;
William Facey from Lancaster; Thomas Hill of Portsmouth; Edward
Jones, the boatswain; Michael Bell of Deptford; John Cavenaugh of
Kilkenny; William Milton from the Azores and James Swilley, the captain's black servant. Burney described them as 'our very best Seamen —
the Stoutest and most healthy people in the ship'. The incident became
known as the massacre of Grass Cove. It was an awful blow to poor
James Burney, the most cultured and sensitive of Furneaux's officers,
to be the first to discover the tragedy and to be responsible for relating
the details to his captain and the rest of the crew. It affected Burney
for the rest of his life. Even after his return to England, he could only

speak of the incident in whispers. But it was a terrible shock to all concerned to lose their colleagues in such a brutal and horrific fashion. Morale on the ship was already at a very low ebb after losing contact with the *Resolution* and we can only sympathise with Tobias Furneaux over the incident. He was not without his faults – as a captain, he could not be expected to measure up to James Cook – but he could not be blamed for the events at Grass Cove, nor could he have been expected to anticipate them. Much later, when further enquiries were made of the Maoris, it transpired that the incident was not premeditated. There had been a quarrel over the usual problems of theft and two Maoris had been shot. The slaughter had been a terrible retribution for the death of the two men.

On 2 December, the crew of the *Adventure* left New Zealand with a heavy heart and set sail westwards for the long voyage home. Cape Horn was rounded with success, and the ship spent some time exploring the southern Atlantic in an unsuccessful search for Cape Bouvet, but the captain wasted little time in getting back to the security of Cape Town. The voyage of exploration was only half completed, but as *Adventure* passes out of the story, the rest of the voyage belongs to the *Resolution* alone.

By December, the *Resolution* was well on her way south towards the Antarctic. By the seventh, the latitude was estimated at 51°30' S and the longitude, as near as they could tell, was 180°. At about seven o'clock, the navigators were directly opposite London, on the antipode of the earth's surface. There was nothing to see but a few penguins and petrels and a great expanse of sea, but the two Forsters and William Wales drank a health to their friends eight thousand miles beneath them on the opposite side of the globe.

On 12 December the first iceberg was sighted and three days later came the first appearance of the pack ice. The *Resolution* continued to the south-east until she crossed the sixtieth parallel, then she set a direct course towards the east. There was some fog, the winds were cold but fair, and she was making good progress, logging sixty to eighty miles in a day. Sometimes the log recorded over a hundred miles per day. The latitude became 65° and as Christmas Day 1773 approached the weather turned colder. Icicles had formed all over the ship's superstructure and sometimes they fell on to the deck from above. The sails became as stiff as boards as the ice froze into them, ropes were stiff to work and unable to run through the icy blocks. Changing a topsail was a bitterly cold and arduous task, but the men of the *Resolution* were used to such conditions and they stuck manfully to their task. It was not just the sailors who were suffering: the botanists were also feeling the strain:

But what unhappy Situation ours must be in these truely inhospitable climates can hardly be expressed by words. The Sun is seldom seen. All is fogg & mist around us: hardly any birds are observed. A few solitary eremitic Whales are now & then seen, & these are all the creatures that will venture to live in this wretched summer *sub Jove frigido* [under a cold sky].

Our food is meat salted, above two years old: & though done with the greatest caution, it is at best but indifferent. All the pease, flower, raisins etc lose something by being so long kept in a Ship excluded from the open Air, are musty & tasteless: in short there is not one comfort in this navigation. The Sea is now tempestuous, the Decks are never dry, all the Ship moist & damp; my Cabin cold & open to the piercing winds, full of unwholesome effluvia & vapours, every thing I touch is moist & mouldy & looks more like a subterraneous mansion for the dead than a habitation for the living. In the Captain's Cabin there are broken panes, the apartment full of currents & smoke, a parcel of damp Sails spread, & a couple of Sailmakers at work, now & then discharging the mephitic Air from the pease & Sower-krout they have eaten, & besides 5 or 6 other people constantly in it: so that it cannot be reckoned one of the most comfortable places neither: if to this we add that there the pitching of the Ship is more felt, than any where else it will clearly appear, that these Expeditions are the most difficult task that could be imposed on poor mortals.[7]

The icebergs became more numerous and it was imperative to keep well clear of them. The most serious problems arose when an ice island shielded the ship from the wind so that she could make no headway and was at the mercy of the currents around the floating island. There was at least one occasion when the ship was caught in the lee of an iceberg and she very nearly came to grief. Cook, for reasons of professional pride, makes light of it, but John Elliott gives a vivid account of the danger and describes the fear on the captain's face. He certainly remembered it as a very close encounter with death:

> But I will here observe that while amongst the Ice Islands we had the most miraculous escape from being every soul lost that ever Men had, and thus it was: The officer of the Watch on deck, while the people was at dinner, had the imprudence to attempt going to windward of an Island of Ice, and from the Ship not going fast and his own fears making her keep too near the Wind, which made her go slower, he got so near that he could get neither one way nor the other, but appeared [to be] going right up on it. And it was twice as high as our Mast heads. In this situation he called up all hands, but to discribe the horrour depicted in every person's face at the awful situation in which we stood is impossible, no less in Cook's than our own, for no one but the officer and a few under his orders had noticed the situation of the Ship. In this situation nothing could be done but to assist the Ship what little we could with the Sails, and wait the event with awful expectation of distruction. Capt Cook ordered light spars to be got ready to push the Ship from the Island if she came so near, but had she come within their reach, we should have been overwhelmed in a moment and every soul drowned. The first stroke would have sent all our Masts overboard, and the next would have knocked the Ship to pieces and drowned us all. We were actually within the backsurge of the Sea from the Island.
>
> But most providentially for us she went clear, her stern just trailing within the Breakers from the Island. Certainly never men had a more narrow escape from the jaws of death.[8]

It was not just the danger of the icebergs that made the voyage so treacherous. The storms were frequent and violent. The intense cold made it very difficult for the sailors to handle the ropes and sails and to respond quickly to changing situations. The deck was covered in ice: it was very slippery and the sea breaking over it made the boards very treacherous underfoot. Climbing the ratlines to work the sails aloft was a terrible task. Even the inside of the ship was not free from the deluge. Johann Forster described one of the storms in graphic detail:

> The Storm & Sea much increased, our Ship is tossed backwards & forwards, up & down the mountainous waves: each summit, from which you may overlook the vast extent of the Ocean, follows again a deep

abyss, where we get hardly light in our Cabins. During night we brought
to & then we felt the rolling infinitely more. At 9 o'clock, there came a
huge mountainous Sea & took the Ship in her middle, & overwhelmed
all her parts with a Deluge. The table in the Steerage, at which we were
sitting, was covered with water, & it put our candle out: the great Cabin
was quite washed over & over by the Sea coming through the Sides of
the Ship. Into my Cabin came the Sea through the Skuttel & wetted all
my bed. I had new sheets laid & the bed rubbed up & dried as well as
could be done, & in this damp bed I turned in, with limbs that had been
free from pain all the day & in very good spirits: but the continual
rolling of the Ship hindered me from Sleeping. Soon did the damp
vapours volatilized by my natural warmth insinuate themselves into
the open pores & penetrate to the fibres, which a few hours ago had
been agitated by pain & caused there new excruciating pains. I did not
sleep all night, my Cabin was now below full of water, & I could not stir
without being in water to my Ankles: fell any thing down, it was most
certainly soaked in the briny Deluge. This disaster however befell my
pillow, whilst I was buzy to rub my poor tortured legs, with a piece of
flanel in order to mitigate at least in some measure the torments, I
thought myself under. The Ocean & the winds raged all night. The
former had no *pacific* aspect, & seemed to be displeased with the pre-
sumption of a few intruding, curious roving puny mortals, who come
into that part of his dominions where he has been undisturbed ever
since the creation: perhaps is he more displeased with their business, of
seeing for land, where never any was. The morning came, I dragged my
crippled limbs out of my bed & ate some breakfast.[9]

On the twenty-second, the latitude was measured as 67°27' S, and
the ship was once again inside the Antarctic Circle. There was no land.
On Christmas Day Cook invited the officers to dine with him. The
petty officers were entertained by one of the lieutenants and the seamen
were given double portions of pudding with a generous allowance of
brandy. The sailors joked that, provided they could have a keg of
brandy, they could die happy on one of the 168 ice islands they could
count around them. Cook decided to head northwards again. On 9
January he logged 161 miles and on the eleventh, which happened to
be Elliott's sixteenth birthday, he was back in more temperate climes
at a latitude of 48° and longitude 120° west of Greenwich. Finding the
ship's position on the surface of the Earth was no problem. 'Indeed our

error can never be great so long as we have so good a guide as Mr Kendall's watch,' wrote Cook, who had by this time become completely converted to the method of the marine chronometer. Supplies of tea and sugar were low, but the crew heaved a great sigh of relief to be in a more temperate zone and a rumour travelled through the ship that they would soon be heading for Cape Horn and bound for home. When pressed on the point, James Cook became characteristically silent. He smiled but said nothing. Then the crew were dismayed to find that they were heading to the south again; supplies of tea and sugar were not essential to exploration. The captain's jaw was set. He had decided that they would spend another year sailing the Pacific Ocean. It was not good news for Johann Forster, who bitterly criticised over-ambitious explorers who did not listen to reason:

> As there is hardly any prospect of meeting with land here it would be best to make the best of this fine gale, & bear down again into 60 & upwards to go round Cape Horn. But we must submit, there are people, who are hardened to all feelings, & will give no ear to the dictates of humanity and reason; false ideas of virtue and good conduct are to them, to leave nothing to chance, & future discoverers, by their perseverance; which costs the lives of poor sailors or at least their healths . . .[10]

He was slightly comforted to see a grey and brown albatross following the ship with a wing span of ten feet. There were minor problems on board: Cook flogged midshipman Loggie, who had lashed out with his knife in a drunken stupor and drawn the blood of two young officers. Generally speaking, the sailors were taking the severe conditions in their stride, but the fresh food was exhausted and the diet was back to salted beef and ship's biscuits. The skies became clear and the weather was holding off. Cook decided to make the most of the fine spell and he headed due south. He entered the Antarctic Circle for the third time on the voyage and continued sailing to the south. On 28 December he logged 103 miles, almost due south. The next day he was still making progress to the south. On the thirtieth, he was stopped by the ice-field again. He had reached the deepest south that it was possible to sail. The latitude was carefully measured and the figure agreed upon was 71°10'.

It is necessary to pause at this point and put the achievement of the *Resolution* into perspective, to stand back and see a tiny wooden vessel surrounded and dwarfed by hundreds of great floating icebergs. Cook's latitude was more than 71° – at most longitudes, this distance to the south is actually a part of the Antarctic continent. He was desperately unfortunate not to be the discoverer of Antarctica, particularly when we consider that he went on effectively to circumnavigate the continent. It was not until 1819 that Edward Bransfield and William Smith sighted the peninsula of Graham Land, at a latitude of 64° S. The *Flying Fish* expedition under Wilkes explored as far as latitude 70° S on 23 March 1839, not far from Cook's position at a longitude of 100°16' W. The two great Antarctic seas, named after Weddel and Ross, were not discovered until the 1860s and 1880s respectively, but this takes us into the era of steam-powered navigation, iron ships and icebreakers. To penetrate as far south as Cook achieved, in an eighteenth-century sailing ship, defies the imagination – he was hundreds of miles inside the Antarctic Circle and a whole century ahead of his time.

There was an eerie silence in that empty sea, broken only by the croaking of the penguins which managed to stay out of sight behind the icebergs. The heavenly display of the southern lights had ceased because there was no longer any night left for them to perform in. The sun circled the skies, dipping close to the horizon in the hours around midnight, but it never set – the perpetual daylight was paid for heavily by the terrible long night of the winter when the sun remained below the horizon for several weeks. The floating icebergs were all around the ship and the danger was very obvious. Some of the bergs were so tall that their tops were covered in cloud and occasionally they would give out a sudden crack like a cannon as the ice melted in the sun. Every man longed for the order to turn the ship, but at the same time every man wanted to savour the feeling of being further south than ever man had penetrated before and in a part of the world which nobody would ever have cause to visit again. The loneliness defies description – the nearest human beings were many thousands of miles away. The emotion of the occasion even reached the impassive James Cook: he admitted that he could not sail an inch further. Even Cook dropped his guard and let his emotions appear in his journal. Not only had he sailed further than any man before, but he knew that he had sailed as far

as it was possible for man to go. They were at the very ends of the
earth:

> I will not say it was impossible any where to get farther to the South,
> but the attempting it would have been a dangerous and rash enterprise
> and what I believe no man in my situation would have thought of. It was
> indeed my opinion as well as the opinion of most on board, that this Ice
> extended quite to the Pole or perhaps joins to some land, to which it
> had been fixed from the creation and that it here, that is to the South of
> this Parallel, where all the Ice we find scatered up and down to the
> North are first form'd and afterwards broke off by gales of Wind or other
> cause and brought to the North by the Currents which we have always
> found to set in that direction in the high Latitudes. As we drew near
> this Ice some Penguins were heard but none seen and but few other
> birds or any other thing that could induce us to think any land was
> near; indeed if there was any land behind this Ice it could afford no
> better retreat for birds or any other animals, than the Ice it self, with
> which it must have been wholy covered. I who had Ambition not only
> to go farther than any one had done before, but as far as it was possible
> for man to go, was not sorry at meeting with this interruption as it in
> some measure relieved us, at least shortned the dangers and hardships
> inseparable with the Navigation of the Southern Polar Rigions; Since
> therefore, we could not proceed one Inch farther to the South, no other
> reason need be assigned for my Tacking and Standing back to the north,
> being at this time in the Latitude of 71°10' S, Longitude 106°54' W. It
> was happy for us that the Weather was Clear when we fell in with this
> Ice and that we discovered it so soon as we did for we had no sooner
> Tacked than we were involved in a thick fog. The Wind was at East and
> blew a fresh breeze, so that we were inabled to return back over that
> space we had already made our selves acquainted with. At Noon the
> Mercury in the Thermometer stood at $32\frac{1}{2}$° [Fahrenheit] and we found
> the air exceeding cold.[11]

At last Cook gave the order to turn the ship. A young midshipman
climbed out past the figure-head of the prancing horse and out along
the bowsprit. He wanted to boast that he had gone further south than
any other man in the world. He turned and waved his hat at the other
sailors. His name was George Vancouver. Little did he or his shipmates
know how much the future would honour him in British Columbia.
George had a rival to his claim, however. The botanist Anders Sparrman

sat at his ease in the rear cabin of the ship as she made the turn. He claimed that the ship had to make way to the south to complete the manœuvre and that therefore he had travelled fractionally further south than any other man on the ship.

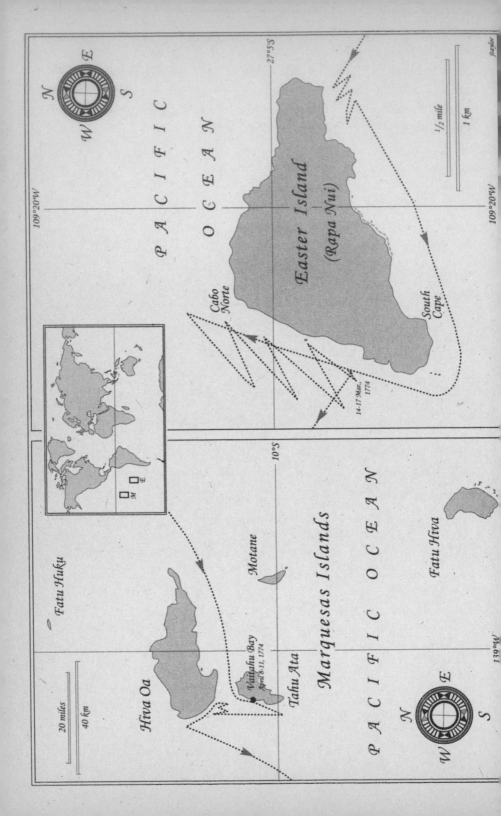

SEVEN

Following the Footsteps

She sped over the waves faster than a javelin, or an arrow that rivals the wind.

Aeneid, x, 247

The voyage to the north was remarkably fast. Strong winds on 8 February carried the *Resolution* 184 miles and she covered another 146 miles the following day. The ice and snow turned to sleet, then to rain and fog. By the eighteenth, the latitude was down to 44° and by the twenty-second the latitude was 38° S and temperatures in the sixties (Fahrenheit) were being recorded. In fact, it could probably be argued that the *Resolution*'s passage, the equivalent distance from the Antarctic Circle to the tropics, was faster than any ship had ever made before her.

The next leg of the voyage was to be a grander version of the first island sweep when the Tongan islands had been rediscovered. Cook made much use of Dalrymple's *Voyages*. The author mentioned a glimpse of the great southern continent seen by Juan Fernandez in the sixteenth century. The sighting was in a longitude close to that of the *Resolution* on her way towards the tropics. Cook was intrigued by the sighting, but he did not put enough confidence in it to spend a lot of time searching – particularly as his ship had been at sea for fourteen weeks and he was badly in need of fresh food and water. Fernandez also discovered the island that is named after him, which lay in a higher latitude off the coast of Peru. The island of Juan Fernandez was well known in Cook's time. It was where the marooned Scotsman Alexander Selkirk had lived alone for five years until, in the year 1708, he was rescued by Captain Woodes Rogers with his ships the *Duchess* and the

Duke. The Rogers voyage was a Bristol venture; he was accompanied by the buccaneer William Dampier, the man responsible for marooning Selkirk on the island in the first place. Two accounts of the Woodes Rogers expedition were published after his return to Bristol and these were read by Daniel Defoe, who based his popular fictional work *Robinson Crusoe* on the experiences of the marooned Scotsman. The position of Juan Fernandez island was therefore well known and this was probably the reason why Cook chose not to seek it out. He headed instead for Easter Island, discovered by the Dutchman Roggeveen on Easter Sunday 1722. It was one of the most isolated and fascinating islands in the Pacific Ocean.

But before the ship reached Easter Island, Cook was taken ill. He developed a fever and a bilious attack. The symptoms were quite different from his illness at Dusky Sound, although the main contributing causes, namely the confined quarters and the lack of fresh food on the long voyage, were exactly the same. It was characteristic of the captain that he tried to hide his illness from the rest of the crew. He ate less food in the hope that nobody would notice his discomfort, but it was soon very obvious to the rest of the crew that their captain was not at all well. The surgeon James Patten gave him strict instructions to stay in bed and confined him to his cabin. On 11 March, when Easter Island was sighted at last, he was still weak and under doctor's orders. The sight of land could not have been more welcome. It was more than a hundred days since the departure from New Zealand, and the great majority of this time had been spent navigating through some of the coldest seas on Earth.

Easter Island is roughly triangular, with a volcanic crater at each of the three corners. It was known to be inhabited and it was no surprise to find the islanders running excitedly along the beach to greet the *Resolution*. The wind had fallen and the ship tacked agonisingly slowly around the island to find a place to anchor. It was nearly three more days before they were able to find a suitable bay. Forster noted what he first took to be a number of standing pillars near the shore, but with the help of the telescope and glasses it was obvious that these were not pillars at all. They were the magnificent and mysterious stone statues for which Easter Island has become justly famous. The explorers were impatient to land and to get a closer look at these Polynesian marvels.

The indigenous population traded readily enough: a piece of cloth purchased forty or fifty pounds of sweet potatoes and there were fruit and vegetables for exchange. One of the Easter Islanders wore a broad-brimmed hat, another had a jacket and a third sported a red silk handkerchief – all evidence of the Spanish ship which had been at Easter Island about four years previously. The Spanish visitation was still fresh in their minds, but a few of the older inhabitants must have remembered Roggeveen's visit in 1722, when the very first contact was made between Easter Island and the outside world. The islanders were very interested in the ship and several men measured the length in arm spans or fathoms, perhaps to compare the size with the Spanish ship from four years ago. There seemed to be a dearth of young women and Cook reasoned correctly that they had been deliberately kept out of the way, probably because of experiences with the Spanish. This did not prevent some of Cook's men from seeking out the women and some limited sexual contact was made in the short duration of the stay.

The great disappointment with Easter Island was the quality of the water – a supply was found but the source was too brackish and the first few barrels had to be thrown away. The natives drank cheerfully from the brackish water and they were even seen drinking sea water but the poor water quality forced the *Resolution* to restrict her visit to only a few days. Cook recovered sufficiently to set foot on shore, but he was not fit enough to explore the island and he delegated the job to Pickersgill and Edgecumbe with a party of sailors and marines. The two Forsters and the astronomer William Wales were to accompany the expedition, a party of twenty-seven in all.

Easter Island raised many questions for the anthropologist. The language was similar to that of Tahiti, with many words in common, and Odiddy was able to redeem himself by communicating tolerably well. Some of the customs were similar, for example, the art of tattooing was practised and the tendency to thieving was rife. The culture was not as advanced as Tahiti, however. The island was poorer, with a population of only about six hundred, but the evidence strongly suggested that the people of both islands had a common ancestry. The only possible explanation was that at some time in the past the ancestors of the current population had crossed the world's greatest ocean from another island thousands of miles to the west. Was it by accident or by design that the voyage had been made? How many generations had passed since the migration? When in Tahiti and also in the Tongan Isles, Cook had discovered that the natives could read the stars and he knew that they could navigate successfully between neighbouring islands. However, was their navigation good enough to find an island only a dozen miles across as far away as Easter Island? Having once reached the island and settled on it, they became a completely isolated community; their knowledge of navigation was not adequate to allow them to leave again.

One of the tasks of the expedition was to examine and measure the mysterious and impressive stone statues. Most of the statues were still standing. With their backs to the sea and impassive frowns on their faces, they were giant brooding figures fashioned from the hips with small hands, large ears and long noses. The islanders claimed that the statues were images of long lost gods from many generations ago. The statues were enormous. Wales measured a fallen statue as twenty-seven feet long and more than eight feet across the shoulders. It was so large that the whole party of nearly thirty people sat in its shade and ate their lunch of fish, fowl and sweet potatoes. Each statue stood on a stone platform called an *ahu* and was capped with a headpiece consisting of a huge cylinder of red stone. Roggeveen, when he discovered Easter Island, had no problems about explaining their construction: he assumed that they were cast on the spot from mud and cement. But the Dutchman was clearly wrong. The statues were not castings at all: they were monoliths, each carved from a single great block of stone quarried by a long-forgotten civilisation of craftsmen.

The islanders had names for their statues. They worshipped them, but they belonged to their ancestors, long before their own time, and they were unable to explain how they came to be there. The Easter Island statues were the strangest and grandest artefacts of all Polynesian art, executed with stone-age tools on a scale that would have graced ancient Egypt. Yet this was the furthest and most isolated outpost of Polynesia. How did the statues come to be on Easter Island? Where had the stone come from? How had the stone been quarried and carved with such primitive tools? How had the great statues been moved from the quarry to the shore? How had the stones been erected in precise rows? How had the huge headpieces been placed so accurately on top of the statues? There were no trees on Easter Island, so the idea of levers and scaffolding seemed to be out of the question. These questions taxed the minds of anthropologists long after Cook and Roggeveen. The facts were so difficult to explain that later visitors thought the statues must be the work of extraterrestrials. Forster gave a detailed description with the names of some of the statues:

In the morning Capt Cook sent Lieut Pickersgill, with a party of Sailors & Marines, to whom Mr Wales, Mr Hodges & I & Sparman associated, into the Country to reconnoitre: we were in all 27 Men. We first stood directly across the country under the high hill, till we came to the other Side of the Island, & there we found 7 stone pillars, 4 of which were still standing, & 3 were overturned perhaps by an Earth-quake. One of the standing ones had lost its hat. These pillars stand on a kind of pedestall or stone elevation: in some places these elevations are made of regularly hewn square stones sitting as regularly & as finely as can be done by a Nation even with good tools. In what manner they contrived these structures is incomprehensible to me, for we saw no tools with them: however the Stone whereof these Walls & Images are made seems not to be of a great hardness for it is red, cavernous, brittle Iron-Stone or Tophus. The Images represent Men to their waist, the Ears are large & they are about 15 foot high & above 5 foot wide, they are ill shaped & have a large solid bonnet on their head like some of the old Egyptian divinities, the bonnet I measured was above 5 foot diam-eter. I observed in the Center on each side a hole, as if the Natives had made these round stones by turning: but we saw afterwards some still larger ones. viz. one 17 feet high, & on the other side the Island one 27 foot high & 9 feet broad below: it was over turned & lay on the powerfull people, more numerous & better civilised: & they are the only monu-ments of their former grandeur. These pillars have all names, & the whole range of pillars near the Sea is commonly called a *Hanga* & they add allways a peculiar Name to it, to particularise or distinguish the Monument & division of the Country. The pillars & walls near the Anchoring & watering place are called *Hanga-roa*, those where we first came to in our march were called Hanga-to-bow, the next *Hanga-Heeve*, *Hanoa mahaga* & so on. The Images or pillars are likewise named. Prob-ably after the Man, to whose memory they were erected. These Names the people know & preserve. The single pillar near *Hange-Roa* is called *Obeena*. Those 7 we met first with, had the following names *Kotomoai*, *Kotomoeeree*, *Koohoo-oo*, *Moraheena*, *Omareeva*, *Ooeenaboo*, *Ooeenapa*. The

large Pillar where we afterward dined is called *Manga-toto*, & so the
Natives preserve the memory of their Ancient Chiefs, for they really
said that they were *Arees*. They make frequently fires under the walls
at the feet of the Stone Images, but we did not see that the Natives
observed any peculiar time to do it in or that they offered anything to
these Images, so that the Author of Roggewein's Voyage must have been
wrong.[1]

The island at one time had supported a more advanced and numerous
population who devoted much of their time and effort to the creation
of the statues, and at one time there had been many trees on the island
for the construction of levers and scaffolding. The astronomer William
Wales came close to the truth when he discovered a quarry on one of
the volcanoes, where he found huge carved stones in various stages of
manufacture. He deduced that the large cylindrical stones mounted on
the heads could be rolled down the slopes to the shore, but he could
not explain how the larger images of the gods themselves could be
moved from the quarry where they were made.

It was a short visit to the strangest island in the Pacific Ocean. Cook
badly needed fresh water and he knew that he still had to sail many
leagues to find it. After only four days, the *Resolution* was back at sea
and sailing to the north-west. The mysterious Easter Island statues
kept their backs silently to the ship and stared impassively inland.
Cook's plan was to try to locate the Marquesas Islands discovered in
1595 by Mendana and Quiros at about 10° south of the Equator. It was
a calculated risk and a journey of well over two thousand miles. He did
not know the exact position of the discovery from two centuries ago,
but he trusted the latitude sufficiently to run down it in the hope of
making a landfall. The captain's illness was causing great concern, not
least to Johann Forster, who hated the thought of having the first
lieutenant in command. Nobody on the ship grouched or grumbled or
was as generally ill-tempered and difficult as Johann Forster – but faced
with the real crisis of a sick captain, he made a very generous gesture
and he offered his pet dog to supply the fresh food needed to aid the
captain's recovery. The pet dog, it is true, had not travelled all the way
from England. It was a Tahitian dog which Forster had adopted as his
pet, but it was still a very commendable gesture on his part. And
Forster's generosity was not in vain. When Cook had fresh meat in his

diet to relieve the monotony of the salted beef and pork, he quickly began to recover.

The Marquesas were sighted after only three weeks of brisk sailing; this was in spite of the very uncertain position. The islands measured only a few miles in length, but the search was made easier by the fact that they were very high, with one of the mountains on Herva Oa rising to a peak of 3,250 feet; they could therefore be seen from a distance of sixty or seventy miles. The four main islands in the group were easily identified from Mendana's description. He had named them San Pedro, La Dominica, Santa Christina and La Magdalena, but Cook was able to establish the native names – Motane, Hiva Oa the largest island, Tuha Ata and Fatu Hiva. The *Resolution* anchored at Tahu Ata and was given the usual Polynesian reception of canoes, which in the Marquesas were fitted with characteristic lateen-matting sails. There were many smaller islands, such as the small, uninhabited rocky island first spotted by the young midshipman Alexander Hood, who had just celebrated his sixteenth birthday. Cook called it Hood's Island.

As with Easter Island, the stay at the Marquesas lasted only a few days, but Odiddy again found that he could communicate well with the inhabitants. Pigs, fruit and vegetables were traded, and most importantly, a good supply of fresh water was found. There was some cheating in the trade and a lot of the usual pilfering. One man stole an iron stanchion from the ship and the marines fired after him. Unfortunately, the fire was too accurate and he was killed by a lucky hit. This was the last thing Cook wanted, but it did have the desired effect of preventing further thefts. The captain was feeling much better after his illness and the next day he tried to locate the son of the dead man to try to make some amends for the accident. Another problem arose after one of the sailors traded some red feathers for a pig. The Marquesians became so keen on the feathers that they refused to trade for anything less. It was an annoying situation, but the watering was almost complete and there was sufficient fresh food to last until the next port of call. Cook described some of the customs and their adornments, but the most interesting aspect of his report is the beauty of the people whom he described as the most attractive race he had yet encountered:

The inhabitants of these Isles are without exception as fine a race of people as any in this Sea or perhaps any whatever; the Men are Tattowed or curiously Marked from head to foot which makes them look dark but the Women (who are but little Tattow'd) youths and young children are as fair as some Europeans, they cloath them Selves with the same sort of cloth and Matting as the Otaheiteans; they wear as Ornaments a kind of Fillit curiously ornamented with Tortice and Mother of Pearl Shills, Feathers etc Round their Necks an Ornament of this form, it is made with Wood on which are stuck with gum a great num[be]r of small red Pease, they also wear bunches of human hair round their legs and arms etc. The Men in general are tall that is about Six feet high, but we saw none so lusty as at Otaheite and the neighbouring isles, nevertheless they are of the same race of People, their language customs &c all tend to prove it.

They dwell in the Vallies and on the sides of the hills near their plantations, their Houses are built after the same manner as at Otaheite, but are much meaner and only covered with the leaves of the bread tree. They have also dwellings or Strong holds on the Summits of the highest Mountains, these we saw by the help of our Glasses, for I did not permit any of our people to go to them for fear of being attack'd by the Natives, whose deposission we were not sufficiently acquainted with.[2]

Charles Clerke wrote:

The inhabitants to speak of them in general are the most beautiful race of people I ever beheld — of a great number of men that fell under my inspection I did not observe a single one either remarkably thin or disagreeably corpulent but they were all in fine Order and exquisitely proportion'd. We saw very few of their Women but what were seen were remarkably fair for the situation of the Country and very beautifull.

He added that the women had long, fine heads of hair, which hung down their backs in a very becoming manner. Forster also commented on their beauty, and the ship's company seemed to be in total agreement on this matter.

The *Resolution* set sail for Tahiti, but a group of two inhabited islands was encountered *en route* and these were added to the map of the Pacific. They were correctly identified as Takeroa and Takapoto, which had been visited at least twice before, once by Roggeveen in 1722 and secondly by Byron in 1764. The islands were mere atolls, but they had sufficient vegetation to support a local community. Forster and his party landed to botanise and to collect a few coconuts, but the inquisitive residents gathered around, carrying spears and other weapons. The islanders made no attempt to attack the landing party, but since it looked as though they could turn nasty at any moment, the British chose to beat a hasty retreat back to the ship. It was known that when Byron landed in 1764 he had to use his firepower and this was probably the reason why the local population was suspicious and unfriendly towards the ship.

Tahiti was reached on 22 April. The visit was informal. One of its purposes was to calibrate the Kendall chronometer by using the longitude of Fort Venus where the transit of Venus had been observed on Cook's previous voyage. The position of Fort Venus was known more accurately than any other point in the Pacific. William Wales immediately set up his instruments for observation. It was the rainy season and he was delayed by thunderstorms, but in due course he was able to confirm that the watch had kept excellent time after the long months at sea. He then used the observations at Tahiti to correct small errors in the position of Easter Island, the Marquesas and the other small islands observed in the later months of the journey.

At our arrival in Matavia Bay in Otahite, the Longitude pointed out by the Watch was 28'38" too far to the West – that is she had lost sence our leaving Queen Charlottes Sound, of her then rate of going $8'34\frac{1}{2}"$; this was in about five Months or some thing more, during which time she had passed through the extremes of both Cold and heat. It was judged that half this Error arose after we left Easter Island by which it appeared that she went better in the Cold than in the hot climates.[3]

The Tahitians were pleased to see the *Resolution* again, and to Cook's surprise he found that supplies were much more plentiful than on his visit in the previous year. The ship was able to stock up well on pigs, fruit and vegetables. For some complex political reason, the Tahitians were planning to attack the neighbouring island of Moorea and they were very busy preparing their fleet of canoes. Cook wanted nothing to do with island politics, but he agreed to the request to review the war fleet and he gave a description of the impressive high-prowed double-hulled canoes:

When we had got Into our boat we took our time to view this fleet, the
Vessels of War consisted of 160 large double Canoes very well equip'd
Man'd and Arm'd altho' I am not sure that they had on board either
their full complement of Fighting men or rowers, I rather think not.
The Chiefs ie all those on the Fighting Stages were drist in their War
habits, that is in a vast quantity of Cloth Turbands, breast Plates and
Helmmets, some of the latter are of such a length as to greatly incumber
the wearer, indeed their whole dress seem'd ill calculated for the day of
Battle and seems to be design'd more for shew than use, be this as
it may they certainly added grandure to the Prospect, as they were
complesant enough to Shew themselves to the best advantage, their
Vessels were decorated with Flags, Streamers &c so that the whole made
a grand and Noble appearence such as was never seen before in this Sea,
their implements of war were Clubs, pikes and Stones. These Canoes
were rainged close along side each other with their heads a Shore and
Sterns to the Sea, the Admirals Vesel was, as near as I could guess, in
the center. Besides these Vesels of War there were 170 Sail of Smaller
double Canoes, all with a little house upon them and rigg'd with Masts
and sails which the others had not, These Canoes must be design'd for
Transporte or Victulars or both and to receive the wounded Men &c;
in the War Canoes were no sort of Provisions whatever. In these 330
Canoes I judged there were no less than 7,760 men a number which
appears incredible especially as we were told that they all belonged to
the districts of Attaholurou and Ahopatea...[4]

They also witnessed a great boat under construction that the Tahitians
had named *Brittania* in honour of their friends. When completed, it
would be the largest boat in the South Seas, and would be powered by
over a hundred paddles. After the review, Cook felt he would like to
have seen the war fleet in action, but that would mean staying on for
several moons. When they heard that he was ready to sail, the Tahitians
offered to bring the battle forward to five days hence, but Cook wisely
decided not to stay and witness the proceedings. It was just as well.
The Tahitians knew that if Cook intervened with his ship's cannon,
then he could divert the course of Polynesian history. Cook was also
aware of this possibility and it was the last thing he wanted to do.

The stay lasted three weeks, during which the red feathers from
Amsterdam Island became a great Tahitian novelty. The most serious
theft was that of a musket stolen from one of the sentries, but with the

permission of the chiefs, Cook had the culprit flogged. Forster recorded that there were twenty or thirty women on board the ship at one point. Cook did not object to the lovemaking, but he had to ban the women because they, too, were involved with the pilfering. The botanists managed to make an excursion into Tahiti to climb the inland mountains and Johann Forster befriended a twelve-year-old boy called Noona who followed him round on his excursions. He wanted to take the boy back with him, but after some consideration Cook refused to take him on board. Sparrman gave a good account of the expedition, describing the wonderful panorama from high in the Tahitian mountains:

We botanists made two expeditions to the top of the wooded mountain summit nearest to the ship. After climbing half the day with our guide, we spent the night in a shelter, or rather under a badly made roof, where we took the precaution of each taking a watch throughout the night in order to assure our safety. In the morning we reached a ridge with precipitous sides, which led to an impenetrable forest. This ridge was not divided from the mountain which we had just climbed and which we had supposed was linked with the high peaks in the interior of the island, but we soon found ourselves confronted by higher and higher mountains divided by ravines and deep valleys with sheer sides. Here one could have found many suitable sites for the erection of those hermitages which in Spain never lack for misanthropic or fanatical inmates. We were enveloped by turns in clouds and mists so that in the end we were thoroughly drenched, but, our elevated goal once attained, we could observe, like Jupiter, the lightning, accompanied by thunder, and the showers passing beneath us. When the sun dispersed the clouds, as a reward for the fatigues we had endured, we were able to see, as if we had been lying like birds, the marvellous spectacle of a limitless ocean upon which floated green islands of varied shape adorned with coconut palms. In the far distance we discerned Huaheine twenty-five leagues away. Our eyes were caught, also, by the view of a part of the Oparri district and the agreeable valley of Matavai, well populated and cultivated, through which we could trace the winding river almost as if it had been on a map. The coconut palms, the giants of the vegetation, appeared in miniature and among them the inhabitants moved about like puppets. In the roadstead we saw the *Resolution*, a dot in the blue immensity, and it astonished us to think that we had voyaged so far on board that little vessel.[5]

On the final night of their stay, the British entertained the Tahitians with a firework display which included 'rockets, serpents and air balloons'. The captain obviously felt that he had gunpowder to spare and the show was enthusiastically received by the islanders. As the ship was ready to leave, the inevitable happened. The gunner's mate, John Marra, jumped ship and swam for the shore; he intended to stay behind with a native girl. He had been promised a house and land as well as a wife – it was a difficult offer for a humble seaman to refuse. He was spotted in the water and a boat was despatched to pick him up; they took him into the boat but he jumped out to escape again. The Irishman was taken a second time. One man who must have sympathised with Marra was Samuel Gibson, corporal of marines – he himself had deserted with one of the local girls on his first visit to Tahiti four years before on the *Endeavour*. Cook was relatively sympathetic. Although he put Marra into irons, he decided not to flog him. The naval discipline was essential, but Cook's confidence as captain had increased since his first voyage and he did not fear any loss of authority. When he came to reflect on the matter, he admitted that Marra was expendable and he might actually have let him stay on Tahiti.

There was a short stop at the island of Huahine, where they were shown another great boat under construction: the number of paddles was given as 144. The next port of call was Raiatea, where Cook wanted to return Odiddy to his own people. Cook's journal describes something of the danger of negotiating the reefs around the island – many of the reefs were long-extinct volcano craters. The rims of the extinct craters made excellent natural harbours where the coral grew up from the rocks beneath the water, but the sea outside tended to be very deep and the gaps in the reef were treacherous entrances to this type of island harbour. Cook described the entrance to the reef at Raiatea: he thought it particularly dangerous where the sea broke with such violence that it was 'frightful to behold'. On this occasion, it took a day and a half to anchor with all the ship's boats at the ready and the men at the ropes of the warping machine.

> After makeing a few trips got before the Channel and with all our sails set and the head way the Ship had acquired, shutt [shot] her in as far as she would go then droped the anchor and tooke in the sails; this is the method of geting into most of the Harbours, which are on the lee side

of these isles, for the channells in general are too narrow to ply in. We were now anchored between the two points of the reef which form the entrance each not more than two thirds the length of a cable from us, and on which the Sea broke with such height and Violence as was frightfull to behold; the sight to people less acquainted with the place would have been terrible.[6]

They were greeted by a strange local custom. Four or five old women appeared, weeping and lamenting and with blood running over their faces and down to their shoulders. The blood was drawn from their foreheads by a strange instrument made from shark's teeth. The captain and his officers were obliged to embrace and console them and they became smeared with blood in the process. The women then went to wash themselves and soon returned 'as cheerful as any of the company'.

The Raiateans were again delighted to see Cook and his crew and they entertained them in the best Polynesian manner. Two theatrical performances were presented. The first production was a very civilised performance. The only actress was Chief Oreo's beautiful daughter Poetua (Poydoa), the lady who had entertained Richard Pickersgill the previous year. Cook noted that she was given many small gifts by her numerous admirers. Poetua's act was followed by a bawdy performance from the male performers. It was William Wales who gave the best account of the proceedings. He even went to the trouble of recording the reaction of part of the audience:

When we got back I found that the Princess Poydoa performed that Evening for the Entertainment of the strangers, as these were my favorite amusements I made scarce more than a hop skip & Jump to the Playhouse where I found she could twist & distort a set of very delicate features with as much dexterity as ever. 'Tis true this did not divert me much; but sufficient Amends were made by some of the Interludes to me, whose tast is not over-&-above delicate. The Concluding Piece, they called Mydiddee Arramy. Which I know not how to translate better than The Child-Coming. The part of the Woman in Labour was performed by a large brawny Man with a great black bushy beard, which was ludicrous enough. He sat on the ground with his legs straight out, between the legs of another who sat behind him and held the labouring man's back hard against his own breast. A large white Cloth was spread over both which was carefully kept close down to the Ground on every side by others who kneeled round them. The farce was carried on for a considerable time with a great many wrigglings and twistings of the body, and Exclamations of Away! Away! Away to perea! (which I dare not translate) untill at length, after a more violent than ordinary struggle out crawled a great lubberly fellow from under the Cloth, and ran across the place between the Audience and Actors, and the he-Mother stradling after, squeezing his breasts between his fingers and dabing them across the youngsters Chaps, & every now & then to heighten the relish of the entertainment mistooke and stroaked them up his backside. On the whole it was conducted with decency enough for a Male Audience, had not Mididdee dragged a great wisp of straw after him which hung by a long string from his Middle. The Women did not however retire even from this part of the Entertainment, or even turn their faces but sat with as demure a Gravity as Judges are said to do when hearing baudy Causes. I asked some who sat round me why they also did not laugh as I did & One of them replied 'Mididdee tooatooy', the aptitude of which expression pleased me as much as the Entertainment itself, because the latter word has exactly the same meaning and is applied in the same manner as the word Impotent is with us.[7]

The iron tiller was stolen from the pinnace and there were other minor thieving problems, but these mishaps were nothing new and the visit was another pleasant and friendly episode. There remained the problem of Odiddy, who still wanted to visit England, but Cook knew that he could not guarantee him a passage back again to the Society Islands and he did not feel at all happy about the welfare of Pacific islanders in European society. After much soul searching, Odiddy agreed to stay at Raiatea. He had been only seven months on the ship, but his friendly and sociable nature had made a good impression on the crew. 'He was a sensible well disposed young Man, and had learn't, all our different distinctions in the Ship – many words etc and had been very happy with us for 7 months,' wrote John Elliott.

The *Resolution* was able to replenish her food stocks for the next stage of the journey, but just as Cook was ready to sail, he received an incredible report that Joseph Banks and Captain Furneaux had landed at the neighbouring island of Huahine only three days ago. The man who brought the report described Banks and Furneaux so well that Cook had no doubt that he was telling the truth. The story was quite incredible but so convincing that Cook was ready to send out a boat straight away to greet them. It was of course perfectly possible that the *Adventure* was still in the Pacific, but how on earth had Joseph Banks managed to arrive? It was a friend of Forster's who told Cook that the whole thing was a lie. The story was a practical joke – it was a side to the Raiatean character that they had never encountered before.

How could the people of the Pacific islands know anything of the world beyond their horizons? What was their conception of the world they lived in? Did they conceive it as a globe, or did they subscribe to a flat-earth theory? They saw the strange large ships appear from a world completely outside their experience. They saw men with pale skins and strange hair. They saw metals, glass and materials unknown in their islands. They saw finely woven cloth, strange powerful shooting sticks and items manufactured from the curious metals, beautiful astronomical instruments and magic spy glasses. They saw things called books full of strange symbols. Yet they knew that the men were mortal and that they would die just as they themselves would die. Chief Oreo's last request was to ask Cook if he would return to see him again and Cook was unable to make any promise. Oreo asked the name of the place where Cook would be buried. Cook thought this a strange request, but it was part of Oreo's culture and soon he would understand the reason for the question. He explained that he lived in the parish of Stepney and that was where he expected to be buried. The name of the unfashionable East End parish was practised and repeated until the Raiateans could make some attempt at pronouncing it. James Cook was never more moved in his life than as the sailors set the sails for the *Resolution* to leave the harbour. The islanders chanted the words 'Stepney Maria no Tootee, Stepney Maria no Tootee'. They had not the faintest conception of what Stepney was like, yet as the *Resolution* sailed into the setting sun the words came out, from the throats of hundreds of the Society Islands' inhabitants, in unison and melancholy sadness.

EIGHT

The New Hebrides

They set off from the harbour and favourable winds filled the sails;
the fleet was carried swiftly over the deep.

Aeneid, v, 32

The process of mapping the world's greatest ocean now commenced in earnest. The sailors were soon reminded that not all the islanders were as warm and friendly as the Society Islanders. Cook headed for the Tonga group just as he had done the previous year, but this time he held a course about one degree to the north of his previous route in the hope of finding undiscovered islands. A small uninhabited island was spotted which turned out to be a collection of even smaller islands with low reefs connected by sand banks and breakers. It made for a dangerous sea and they were well aware that sharp rocks lay hidden beneath the water. They named the islands after Lord Palmerston, one of the Lords of the Admiralty. Four days later, there was a false call of land when a cloud formation was sighted, but only an hour later real land was seen from the mast head. This time, they had discovered a long island with people armed with slings and spears running along the shore to keep up with the ship. The *Resolution* hove to and Cook sent out two boats to investigate; he commanded one himself and put Pickersgill in charge of the other. The inhabitants disappeared into the woods. They seemed hostile and it was agreed that they should be treated with caution. The precautions were just as well, for a man appeared suddenly from the wood and slung a stone, a lump of coral rock, some forty yards to strike Anders Sparrman on the left forearm. In the confusion that followed, muskets were fired without orders from the captain. This was not what Cook wished. His policy was always to befriend the locals and to use firepower only in an emergency if things got out of hand. He decided to retreat and to try landing at another part of the island.

About four miles along the coast, he found a small beach. It was deserted, but four canoes had been left there. He landed and put some small tokens in the canoes, hoping that the owners would find them. The gesture was not appreciated. A few minutes later, the islanders came rushing out of the bush 'with the ferocity of a wild boar', their leader throwing darts at the intruders. The men wore feathers and were daubed with a black greasy substance, which was also smeared on their spears. Cook ordered the muskets to be fired into the air, but the musket fire only angered the islanders and they became more determined than ever to drive off the pale-faced invaders. The second boat arrived on the scene with Pickersgill and the botanists, the Forsters and Anders Sparrman – they had managed to collect a few meagre specimens, but they too had been unable to parley with the indigenous population. Cook decided it was not worth spending any more time there and he branded his latest find with the name of 'Savage Island'. The native name was Niue.

Cook wanted a second look at the Tongan Islands and he correctly reasoned that his current track, about one degree to the north of the course he had taken the previous year, would take him through the other islands in the group. Sure enough, on 25 June more small islands were seen. The first four were joined by a reef of rocks. They were an obvious danger but they could easily be given a wide clearance and the next day a safe passage was found through them. Gentle breezes and pleasant weather brought them to the island of Nomuka which Cook identified as another member of the island group discovered by Tasman (who called it Rotterdam). Here they were received with great courtesy and conducted to a pond of brackish but adequate water – it was the same watering point as Tasman had used many years before. The residents were friendly and they willingly helped to roll the casks of water from the well to the boat.

The surgeon, James Patten, undertook an expedition of his own to shoot wildfowl. He was late returning and when the tide ebbed out of the landing place Cook had to leave him stranded on the island. All was going well until a man snatched the surgeon's musket from him. It was another example of the natural and uncontrollable instinct of the Polynesian people to covet and steal any item which took their fancy. The thief could not have known that it was a lethal weapon he had stolen and there was no way in which he could fire it without a knowledge of its workings, but he knew something about its powers for he had seen Patten using it to shoot the birds. When Cook discovered the theft, he obviously wanted to recover the musket, but he saw no reason to make a great scene about the incident. Then the other islanders, seeing that the thief seemed to have got away with his crime, became bolder and tried to steal other items from the boats. One man got hold of the lead line and pulled it so hard that the line broke. In spite of warning fire from the muskets, he coolly went around to the other side of the ship with the intent of stealing the second lead line. The watering of the ship continued, but the islanders became less helpful and they hovered around with the intent of stealing and causing mischief. Some of the cooper's tools went missing and then unfortunately a second musket was stolen – this time that of Lieutenant Clerke. It was now essential that both the firearms be returned. It was a job for the marines. Muskets were fired and the thieves were wounded. They fled from the scene but both the muskets were duly returned.

An adze was also stolen and Cook explained to an elderly and very vociferous woman that he wanted it back. She gave him the rough edge of her tongue. Cook could hardly understand a word, but she understood well enough what he wanted. She went off with three or four other women and soon returned with the stolen item, but she made off before Cook could give her a present to show his thanks. Then the reverse happened. The woman returned with a present for the captain in the form of a young and beautiful girl with whom he was invited to take his pleasure.

This presented a very difficult situation for Captain Cook. It was not his policy to take advantage of the local girls, even when they were willing and presented to him as a special favour. He could have pretended to make love to her, privately in his cabin or somewhere on shore, but this would only offend the girl and rumours would soon spread around the ship that the captain was too old and incapable of enjoying the fair sex. There was an even more difficult reason. He had strongly discouraged having the girls on board ship because it

encouraged theft and pilfering. For him to take a girl and to deny the
pleasure to the other men would therefore make him seem a hypocrite.
He made the weak and false excuse that he had no shirt or nail to give
her, but they knew this was a lie and they agreed instead to accept
credit on her behalf. His own words express his dilemma pretty accurately:

> For I was no sooner returned from the Pond the first time I landed than
> this woman and a man presented to me a young woman and gave me to
> understand she was at my service. Miss. who probably had received her
> instructions, I found wanted by way of Handsel [an advance payment]
> a Shirt or a Nail, neither the one nor the other I had to give without
> giving her the Shirt on my back which I was not in a humour to do. I
> soon made them sencible of my Poverty and thought by that means to
> have come of with flying Colours but I was misstaken for I was made to
> understand I might retire with her on credit, this not suteing me niether
> the old Lady began first to argue with me and when that fail'd she
> abused me, I understood very little of what she said, but her actions
> were expressive enough and shew'd that her words were to this effect,
> Sneering in my face and saying, what sort of a man are you thus to refuse
> the embraces of so fine a young Woman, for the girl certainly did not
> [want] beauty which I could however withstand, but the abuse of the
> old Woman I could not and therefore hastned into the Boat, they then
> would needs have me take the girl on board with me, but this could not
> be done as I had come to a Resolution not to suffer a Woman to come on
> board the Ship on any pretence what ever and had given strict orders to
> the officers to that purpose for reasons which I shall mention in a nother
> place.

Elliott recorded that 'It has always been supposed that Cook himself
never had any connection with any of our fair friends. I have often seen
them jeer and laugh at him, calling him *Old*, and good for nothing.'
This was written at Tahiti, but we must remember to allow for the
fact that the close threesome of Elliott, Hood and Vancouver were all
in their teens and from their viewpoint Cook was an elderly man well
past the age to be interested in girls. In point of fact, James Cook had
left his wife pregnant when he left England and she became pregnant
again after his return. The adolescents were wrong to imply that their
captain was too old for sexual relations. The attitude of the midshipmen

did not trouble him in the least. He knew his duty and his only option was to stick with his principles.

Then came another incident. Amid all the commotion of lost muskets and nubile South Sea maidens, the chronometer, which had kept such good time throughout the whole voyage, had stopped. It was not the fault of the instrument itself. Nobody had remembered to wind it. The chronometer was the responsibility of William Wales and the elder Forster's garbled version put the whole of the blame on the astronomer:

> When this Morning the Astronomer wanted to compare his watch with Kendal's Timekeeper, he found that it was standing, which at first amazed him very much: but when the Capt said to him, he should try to set it again a going, he found that he forgot to wind up the watch the day before. He then wanted to lay the fault upon the Capt & the first Lieut, who were not on board at the ordinary time of winding up the watch at 12 o'clock, but the Capt told, he had left on purpose the key in the Lock & he might have called another Officer for to sign the Name, & the first Lieut had left his key with the first Mate, but the Astronomer had not asked for it; & besides we returned at 2 o'clock all to dinner, when it was still time enough to wind the watch up, for it was not down then after several hours after this time & we did not return a shore before 4 o'clock was passed. Thus it was owing to mere neglect. The watch was wound up & set a going from a new departure & the time ascertained by observations.[2]

Forster was too harsh in his condemnation of the astronomer, but his relations with William Wales, as with many others of the crew, had gradually deteriorated since the beginning of the voyage. The stopping of the watch was not a major calamity. Wales had kept very careful records and he knew the longitude pretty accurately from his astronomical observations. He was quickly able to reset it to the correct Greenwich time. Forster, having vented some of his frustration on the astronomer, then went on to complain about the captain. The botanists were not allowed to make a landing without the consent of James Cook. This was doubtless for reasons of safety, but it meant that the collectors frequently had very short notice of an opportunity to go ashore and consequently when permission was given they were not ready with their books and equipment. It was the rainy season and Forster com-

plained for the umpteenth time that his cabin and bedding were wet
through. The discomfort was nothing compared to wet bedding in the
Antarctic, but he extended his grouch to the community at large and
the lack of appreciation for scientific knowledge:

> The Isle of *Tofooa* we looked at, without sending a boat ashore, where I
> missed again an opportunity of getting new plants & all the money of
> the public is as if it were thrown away & my mission absolutely made
> useless for want of opportunities to collect new plants, which grow
> plentifully in the new Isles. Though they are within reach; either we
> stay but a day or 2 on one place, go late ashore, come early off again, are
> hindered to ramble about by the carelessness of people in guarding their
> Arms, have no opportunity of going ashore where something might be
> collected; And avoid to go to such places, where fresh provisions for the
> Ship & plants for me might be gotten, viz: Amsterdam was postponed &
> a little barren rock *Tofooa*, thought more worthy of examination, & after
> all we stared at it & even did not ascertain whether it has a Volcano or
> not, for which purpose we however came. People who know nothing of
> Sciences & hate them, never care whether they are enlarged & know-
> ledge increases or not. This Age only cares to make the most money; &
> enquires after the means of scraping by all ways something together.
> What good can arise from seeing 2 or 3 Isles more in the South-Sea?
> without knowing its products & the Nature of its Soil & the Disposition
> of its Inhabitants: all which cannot be learned by staring afar off at an
> Isle.[3]

James Cook wisely chose to ignore his critics. His plan was to sail to
the north-west, where he knew that other islands had been sighted in
the past. In 1768 the French explorer Bougainville had sailed through
a group of islands which he had correctly identified with a much earlier
Spanish expedition – the first island which Bougainville sighted he
called Aurora, thinking that it could be an outlying part of the great
southern continent – a very optimistic assumption considering that
the latitude was only 15°. It was part of the archipelago now known as
the New Hebrides, of which the largest island was Vanuatu, named
Espiritu Santo by the Spanish. In 1595 the Spanish had made a premature attempt to found a colony in this remote part of the Pacific.
The leader of the expedition was Mendana, with two Spanish galleons,
and it was on the same voyage as his discovery of the Marquesas islands.

Mendana's original plan was to sail further west to the Solomon Isles, which he himself had discovered on his earlier expedition in 1568. Before he reached the Solomons, however, Mendana discovered an island that he decided would be just as suitable for the foundation of his colony and he called the island Santa Cruz. The sequel was a very tragic story: the colony of Santa Cruz lasted only two months and many of the colonists, including Mendana himself, died attempting to create a settlement. The second galleon in his convoy ignored the efforts at Santa Cruz but went on to an even worse fate. It managed to find the Solomon Isles but unfortunately perished with all her crew on the island of San Cristobel. The fate of the Spanish expedition would have remained unknown had it not been for Pedro de Quiros, who was Mendana's pilot and the second in command of his ship. Quiros managed to rescue a hundred famished survivors from Santa Cruz and he eventually got them safely back to Manila.

The dream of founding a Spanish colony was not abandoned. Ten years later, in 1606, Quiros himself commanded an expedition of two galleons sailing from Peru, and his second in command was another great navigator, Luis Vaes de Torres. The galleons sailed through the Tuamotus archipelago and continued westwards for two months. It was perhaps no great surprise that the ships could not find the island of Santa Cruz again, but Quiros discovered a larger island which he called Australia del Espiritu Santo. It was the largest island in the group which Cook named the New Hebrides. The reason for the prefix 'Australia' was that the islands were large and mountainous, they stood high out of the sea and Quiros was convinced that they were just offshore from the great southern continent, the *Terra Australis Incognita*. It soon became obvious that Quiros had not discovered a new continent and the second attempt at founding a Spanish colony was also abandoned. Quiros then took a long route back home, sailing northwards as far as 38°, but eventually he got his ship back to South America. Torres, however, with the second Spanish galleon of the expedition, decided to sail westwards and head for the Philippines. The winds were against him and he was forced to sail to the south of New Guinea. This was how he came accidentally to discover the straits between New Guinea and Australia that bear his name.

The premature attempts at founding a Spanish colony were so many

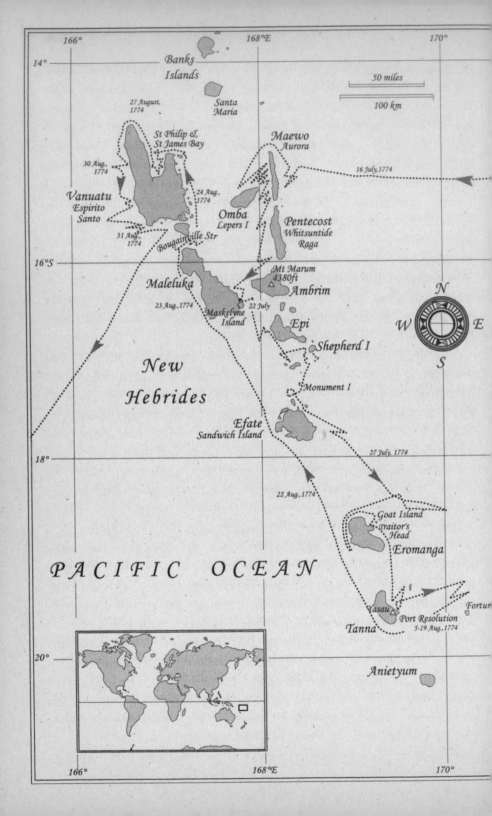

generations in the past that an air of mystery and legend surrounded the islands. Cook was in no doubt, however, that they existed and his next task was to sail in the centuries-old wake of the Spanish galleons and to try and find the same landfalls. For nearly three weeks the *Resolution* sailed to the west in search of the islands. On 16 July, land was seen ahead but the weather changed for the worse; the ship was blown back by the gale and she had to ride out the storm before making the final approach. The next day, the visibility improved and there was a spectacular vista of land ahead of them. There were many islands in sight; they were high and mountainous with other islands visible behind them. It was easy to see why Quiros thought he had discovered the fringes of a great continent. The nearest island was identified as the one that Bougainville called Aurora, and to the south of it was the island he had called Pentecost. The local names were found to be Maewo and Raga. Cook did not expect to find a continent, but the islands were of a good size. Maewo and its neighbour both measured about thirty miles in length and behind them could be seen the largest islands in the group, Espiritu Santo and Malekula. They were both very irregular in shape, but when Cook got around to surveying them he found that they measured about sixty by thirty and fifty by twenty miles respectively.

Cook was now in his element. He set about the major task of charting the whole island group. The *Resolution* rounded the north cape of Maewo to get to the lee side of the island and to discover the island of Omba hidden behind it. This island was recognized as the one that Bougainville called the Isle of Lepers on account of the leprous appearance of the inhabitants. Cook tacked laboriously through the straits between them. The island of Espiritu Santo, where Quiros had tried to found his colony, lay dominating the skyline to the west but he chose to leave the large island until the end and to work his way instead along the chain of islands which could be seen stretching away to the south.

He sailed along the west coast of Whitsuntide or Pentecost Island to reach Ambrim. This island, although it was less than twenty miles at its maximum dimension, boasted two active volcanoes, both of which were taller than the highest peaks in England and the highest, Mount Marum at 4,380 feet and rising directly from sea level, was almost as

high as Ben Nevis, the highest point in the British Isles. The summit
was covered in cloud. Judging by the number of fires, it seemed to be a
very populous island. But this was misleading – the fires were not man-
made, and much of the cloud was in fact smoke and vapour from the
volcano. The fires were red-hot lava running down the slopes and into
the steaming sea.

To the west lay the coast of Malekula Island. Cook tried wherever
possible to find the local name for the islands, but the many small and
unnamed islands gave him the opportunity to honour his friends and
patrons. Shepherd Island, offshore from Epi, was named after Anthony
Shepherd, a Cambridge astronomer – it was the second island to be
named after an astronomer, for William Wales chose the name Maskelyne Island for a small island near Malekula. A tiny island, little
more than a tall rock stained white with bird droppings, was named
Monument Island. The next island was Efate, which Cook called Sandwich Island after the Lord of the Admiralty. To the south-east lay two
more goodly sized islands with a few lesser islands scattered around
them and forming the southern extent of the group. A small offshore
island with a peaked saddle was named Goat Island. The wind dropped
and progress was slow, but a sudden squall on the approach to Eromanga
drove the *Resolution* out to sea. She soon made up the ground and an
attempt at a landing was made. To the south was the island of Tana
and another island called Anietyum was visible further to the south
again. It was the most southerly of the group.

The method used to chart the coast was by means of 'ship stations'.
The ship would typically sail about two miles offshore and anchor at a
good vantage point. Bearings would be taken of all the visible capes,
headlands and other features and then sketches were made from the
ship. The latitude and longitude of the 'ship station' was measured and
then the ship sailed to the next station. The log line could be used to
determine the distance travelled by dead reckoning and the lead line
used to determine depth in fathoms. The latter had to be corrected
to give the depth of water at low tide. This was difficult to measure
unless the ship could anchor for a complete cycle of the tide. If the ship
sailed overnight, then one or more coastal features must still be visible
the next morning to provide datum for the next station. Azimuth
bearings could be taken with the ship's compass, but Cook preferred

to use the sextant because it gave him much more accurate angles and it could also measure vertical angles to estimate the heights of the hills.

George Forster was quick to appreciate the dangers of charting new lands, and the risks that the explorers had to take in order to get accurate information for the maps and charts. When they were at Shepherd Island, to the south-east of Epi, the wind dropped, the ship was becalmed and was swept along at the mercy of the currents:

the darkness of the night, and several broken rocks close to us on all sides, rendered our situation extremely critical. The navigator, who means to explore new islands, and give an accurate account of their position, is often in danger of losing his ship. It is impossible for him to form a just conception of the coast, without approaching close to it, but he must necessarily be exposed to the dangers of a sudden storm, a sunken rock or a swift current, which are sufficient, in a few moments, to destroy all his hopes of glory. Prudence and caution are very necessary in the conduct of every great enterprise, but it seems, that in a voyage of discovery, as in every undertaking of consequence, a certain degree of rashness, and reliance on good fortune, become the principal roads to fame, by being crowned with great and undeserved success.[4]

At Malekula, hundreds of the indigenous population were seen running excitedly along the coast and following the ship, and as the *Resolution* approached for a landing they came out in their canoes to greet the newcomers. It was immediately obvious that they were a different race from the Polynesian people seen on the Society and Tonga Islands. They were of smaller stature, with darker skins and woolly hair, and the men were bearded, with thick lips and flat noses. Their skulls were elongated, they had low brows and Johann Forster thought them more apelike than their Tongan neighbours. The men wore a cloth band wrapped tightly around the waist and their only other garment was a wrapper to protect the penis. Made from a banana leaf dyed with coconut oil and tied by a string to the tight waistband, the wrapper offered only minimal protection and did not cover the testicles — presumably it also served as some form of male genital display to impress the females. Cook described the people as ugly

and ill proportioned. Johann Forster disagreed and found them well
proportioned. When he saw the women, however, he described them
as the most disagreeable creatures he had ever seen. They wore little
more than the men, simply short grass aprons around their waists, and
they daubed their faces with a red ochre which to European eyes did
nothing to enhance their beauty. No doubt the beauty was in the eye
of the beholder. Their appearance was deceptive and the British had
not had time to adjust their minds to a different physique. When they
came to make closer contact, George Forster noticed that the people
were 'full of great sprightliness and express a quick comprehension'.
In fact, they found the islanders to be a happy people fond of music
and dancing. In the fine evenings and bright moonlight, songs could be
heard sung in high-pitched voices as they danced to the beating of their
upright ancestral drums. When they were given mirrors in exchange
for their produce, they proved as vain as any other race and beheld
their image in the glass with delight.

It became apparent that the Pacific Islands were peopled by at
least two races. The Polynesians, with whom the explorers were very
familiar, occupied the middle and eastern ocean, but the western islands
were largely populated by the Melanesian races. The boundary between
the two peoples wove in a complex and confusing pattern around the
island archipelagos, sometimes with both peoples living on the same
island. The explorers had crossed the boundary to encounter the Melanesian race, but they were later to discover that both races cohabited
on the island of Tanna to the south.

The first landing was made on the island of Malekula. A good number
of canoes came out to the ship and Cook was nervous because the
islanders carried their weapons with them. In the early stages, one man
drew his bow and pointed his arrow at the boat keeper. The arrow was
smeared with a green gum, which looked as though it could have been
poison. Cook warned the man off but this did not deter him and he
therefore fired small shot to scare him off. By this time, the whole ship
was crawling from the topmast to the chains with climbing Malekulans
and Cook felt they were getting out of hand. Following his usual
procedure, he ordered a shot from the four-pound cannon. This had
the desired effect: the loud report frightened the islanders and they
scrambled quickly down the rigging and ran from the ship in terror.

Some jumped right out of their canoes and swam ashore. It did nothing to help the trade.

The next morning, when Cook landed at nine, he estimated that four or five hundred men were assembled with spears, bows and arrows. They watched the newcomers inquisitively but made no opposition to the landing. He managed to set foot on shore and to cut wood for the ship, but he made sure that his party was protected by the marines. He was offered a few pigs and fowls, some yams, plenty of coconuts and breadfruit, but little or no fresh fruit. For some reason, the trade he wanted was not forthcoming and he therefore decided not to stay but to try his luck on the other islands.

No attempt to land was made at the island of Efate, but the island of Eromanga looked promising and the ship sailed anti-clockwise around the island, looking for a suitable place to land. The natives were soon seen following the *Resolution* around the coast. A heavy surf delayed the first attempt to land and by the time the ship arrived at a promising beach, a large crowd had gathered to greet them. There were several hundred men, all fully armed, waiting on shore for the strangers to land. The chief arranged his men in a great semicircle around the beach. Cook held a green palm in his hand and offered trinkets and made signs that he needed wood and water. He asked for food and was ceremoniously offered a yam and a few coconuts. The chief motioned Cook to haul his boat onshore, but there was something suspicious about the whole situation. When Cook stepped out on to the beach, he sensed a trap. The chief seemed to be issuing instructions to his warriors all the time. Once Cook had set foot onshore, he felt very uneasy. He decided to retreat and a plank was put out for him to return to the boat. It was then that things suddenly turned very nasty:

the gang-board having been put out for me to come in some seized hold of it while others snatched hold of the Oars, upon my pointing a musquet at them they in some measure desisted, but return'd again in an instant seemingly ditermined to haul the boat up upon Shore; at the head of this party was the Chief, and the others who had not room to come to the boat stood ready with their darts and bows and arrows in hand to support them: our own safety became now the only consideration and yet I was very loath to fire upon such a Multitude and resolved to make the chief a lone fall a Victim to his own treachery, but my Musquet at this critical moment refused to perform its part and made it absolutely necessary for me to give orders to fire as they now began to Shoot their Arrows and throw darts and Stones at us, the first discharge threw them into Confusion but another discharge was hardly sufficient to drive them of the beach and after all they continued to throw Stones from behind the trees and bushes and one woud peep out now and then and throw a dart, four laid to all appearence dead on the shore, but two of them after wards cript into the bushes, happy for many of these poor people not half our Musquets would go of otherwise many more must have fallen. We had one man wounded in the Cheek with a Dart the point of which was as thick as ones finger and yet it entered above two Inches which shews the force with which it must have been thrown. An arrow struck Mr Gilberts naked breast but hardly penetrated the skin, he was in the Cutter about 30 yards from the shore. After all was over we return'd on board and I orderd the Anchor to be hove up in order to anchoring nearer the landing place, while this was doing several of the Islanders assembled on a low rocky point and there displayed two Oars we had lost in the Scuffle. I looked upon this as a Sign of Submission. I was nevertheless prevailed upon to fire a four pound Shott at them to let them see the effect of our great guns, the ball fell short but frightned them so much that not one afterwards appeared, the Oars they left standing up against the Bushes.[5]

It was a very close encounter and some of the officers, such as John Elliott, were absolutely correct when they were convinced that Cook was in great danger of his life. He wisely decided not to stay any longer on Eromanga, but there was a flat calm and there was no wind to take the ship out of the harbour. The ship's boats were launched and, watched from behind the trees by hundreds of armed warriors, the *Resolution* was laboriously pulled out of the harbour. Cook felt that the invitation to land had been a trap and thus he called the headland at the edge of the bay Traitor's Head.

Cook was very puzzled by his reception in the New Hebrides. Where the people of the Society Islands and the Friendly Islands had massed excitedly around the ship and quickly grasped the idea of trade, the Melanesians had made strange symbolic offerings and appeared to be afraid of the newcomers on their shores. It is unfortunate that the Melanesian people have no written record, for there are many ways in which a primitive people could interpret the event. A large ship appears silently out of the mist. A few may have glimpsed Bougainville's ship about six years ago, but for the great majority the *Resolution* was quite unlike anything they had ever seen before. The memory of Quiros's visit may have remained in the folklore memories. However, it was so long ago that if the tale was still alive then it was very distorted after being told and retold over many generations. What the islanders saw was an alien craft peopled by a race of pale men wearing strange garments, with magic fire sticks carrying their own thunder and with miraculous artefacts. They saw a ship full of curious objects outside their comprehension. Why did the men go round collecting plants and examining the rocks? Why did they want to investigate the sacred volcanoes? Why were the volcanoes erupting with far more violence than usual? The Melanesians thought the ghostly new arrivals were the spirits of their ancestors. Were they ghosts or were they gods? Either way, they needed only a spiritual offering and not a shipload of island hogs to feed them. Cook was puzzled. He knew that he had found a different race of people, but he never found out the truth about what the islanders thought of him.

There were a few incidents between islands. At one point a fire broke out in what they feared was the sail room and in a part of the ship not far from the powder magazine. Fire on board ship was a serious problem. If the gunpowder caught fire, then the whole ship would explode, and if this happened the *Adventure* would not be there to pick up the pieces. Luckily the source turned out to be in a neighbouring room where an oil lamp had set light to a piece of Tahitian cloth. It raised a lot of smoke, but it was quickly brought under control and it is significant that Cook did not choose to record the incident for his superiors to read in his log. Another problem that arose was a case of food poisoning from an unfamiliar species of red fish. It caused a lot of discomfort and vomiting but everybody recovered after a few days. There was an experiment to determine whether or not the Malekulan arrowheads were poisoned. One of the dogs was deliberately wounded and the poison from the arrow was applied to the wound to establish what effect it had. The dog remained very sprightly and did not seem to notice any discomfort. On the approach to Eromanga, one of the ship's rails broke and a marine, William Wedgeborough, who was drawing water to wash the decks, fell overboard. These were shark-infested waters, but luckily he was spotted and brought back on board, where his colleagues revived him with rum.

At sunset, another island had been sighted to the south and Cook decided to try his chances there. It was a spectacular island with lush vegetation, rising high and steep out of the sea, but the most striking thing about it was the volcano which at the time was very active, belching fire and smoke high into the atmosphere. Great peals of thunder rolled out across the water as the molten rock in the earth's crust pressed to escape from the crater of the angry volcano of Yasau. The approach to the island by night was a spectacular sight that far exceeded the puny firework display at the Society Islands. The skies were full of red, orange and yellow flames as molten rocks were thrown into the air by the eruption. On the slopes of the volcano a river of molten lava flowed down to the sea. The ash rained down from the sky and when morning broke the deck of the ship was covered with a fine white powder.

But the *Resolution* sailed on. Fresh supplies were always needed and on the morning of 6 August a landing place was found. The light winds made the progress slow and the locals therefore had plenty of warning of the approach. By the time a landing place had been found, they were massed on the shore by the hundred, left and right – all armed with clubs, bow and arrow, spears and stones. It seemed to be a repeat performance of the two previous landings.

Cook made ready to land. He carefully placed the ship where the great guns could be used if necessary, but he took his green olive branch as a sign of peace. Once again, the usual consort of canoes came out to trade and soon the natives were in the rigging and climbing all over the ship, trying to pilfer anything that was not tied down. When they became bolder, Cook once again tried to frighten them off by firing muskets into the air. Once again, when this had no effect, he fired a four-pound cannon ball and once again the report was loud enough to send them scurrying away from the ship.

The atmosphere was made tenser by the rumbling of the volcano, which gave out an explosion every four to five minutes and kept throwing columns of smoke up into the sky. The air smelt of sulphur and ash was falling from above. Cook made signs that he wanted them to lay aside their weapons. He found that he had an ally in an elderly man, whom he found was called Paowang. But the situation seemed very dangerous and Cook approached with the utmost caution. He was met by a ceremonial offering of yams, plantains and breadfruit. The tension eased a little and the feared hostilities did not develop. He indicated his need for wood and water and the island chief allowed him to fill the casks. The watering was performed with a strong guard of marines as escort in case the situation got out of hand.

The British returned to the ship and an uneasy peace held out through the night. The next day saw signs of improvement. A few of the natives had left their arms behind and the ship was treated with more respect than on the first day. Paowang brought coconuts out in his canoe. He was rewarded with a mirror and as he admired his own image he was so delighted that he failed to notice his canoe drifting out to sea – he had great problems getting back into the bay. A small pig was traded and the crew made sure the trader was suitably rewarded, but the much-needed flow of provisions did not materialise. The scientists were as usual very keen to explore the island. They ventured out to get a closer look at the volcano, but they were stopped and directed down to the shore by the natives. The volcano with its active eruptions held a prominent place in their religious beliefs, but because of the language barrier it was impossible to work out its true significance. Hot springs and steaming pools were found on the slopes of the volcano and temperatures of 170 and 180° Fahrenheit were measured. In one case, the water was boiling at almost 210°. One of the natives cheated Johann Forster by giving him a bunch of leaves that were supposed to contain nutmegs, but there was no fruit with the leaves. Charles Clerk was present and tried to prevent the elder Forster from 'kicking up a cabal' (making a great fuss), but his interference only caused a greater 'cabal' as the older man disliked taking orders from the young lieutenant:

> I made signs to be angry & spit out as if it were a bad thing: then the other Indians rebuked him & he stept back: Lieut Clarck who came to it said I was kicking up a Cabal, as his Expression was, & desired me not to do it, I told, it was no Cabal to tell a Man, he had done wrong, when he did so, & that the Natives knew themselves the thing to be so, & therefore could I never think this to be a Cabal. He said he would make me do as he pleased. I said I never had been put under his or any bodies

orders & were not responsible for my conduct to him, which was besides
harmless. He said, if I did not obey his orders, he would give orders to
the Sentry to shoot me. I said I would acquaint the Captain, that he
assumed an authority, which never was given to him.[6]

They both went to take their dispute to the captain. Cook was not
prepared to take sides on the issue, but he told Forster that he must
abide by the regulations. Forster replied that this was not the issue.
The point was whether or not Lieutenant Clerk had the authority to
meddle in his own affairs and tell him what to do. Forster demanded
that Cook tell his officers they could not give him orders. Cook replied
that he would do no such thing. Forster did not give up so easily. He
continued letting off steam with his grievance:

> then said I, I must be afraid to go ashore because every petty Chap in
> the Ship, even a coxswain, would pretend to give me orders; & so said
> he, you must be under their orders. I desired to give me this declaration
> under his handwriting, but he refused. I told him. He durst not be
> ashamed to write what he was not ashamed to say, & I believed he was
> afraid it would serve against him: he said he was not. Why then will you
> not do it, replied I. At last we gave up our dispute; but this Specimen
> only shall serve to shew, what a hard thing it is, to be on board a Man
> of war, where every petty Officer or boy pretends to command Men, that
> never were intended to be controuled by such inconsiderable beings: the
> greater part of these people are so used to command & to bashaw it over
> other people, that no Man of honour will for the future venture to go
> on any Errand on board His Majesties Ship, for fear to be ill treated by
> these imperious people, who cringe ashore for preferment, &' are often
> thought to be civil, nay polite; but as soon as they return to their
> Element the Sea, they are as rough & boisterous as it. There may be a
> few Exceptions to it, but I have reason to believe, but few.[7]

William Wales claimed that Forster was rebuked by Clerk for 'spur-
ning with his foot and spitting in the face' of the Melanesian. George
Forster also wrote about the incident. He was anxious to show his
father in the best possible light and he accepted that his father ques-
tioned Clerke's authority to order him about, but he claimed that the
dispute was short lived and that the two men quickly made up their
differences. 'That good humoured man, Clerke, may have been
extremely waspish at the time,' said George, 'but both Clerke and my

father have since laughed at the violent heat to which they suffered such trifles to mislead them. Where is the man that is not sometimes run away with by passion?'

This was an isolated incident; the care and precautions taken at Tanna were beginning to take effect. Both sides relaxed and the islanders, when they saw the sailors collecting coconuts, helped by climbing the trees and throwing down the nuts. They were so eager that it was necessary only to point at a tree. They would climb it like a squirrel and clear the tree in an instant, not expecting to gain any reward for their labour. Cook mellowed in his opinion of the people. He admitted to himself that his visit was an invasion of the island since his crew wandered at liberty all over their property and took what was needed by way of food, wood and water.

Then, just as the situation seemed to be stable, disaster struck. One of the marines shot and killed an islander. It was the very thing that Cook wanted to avoid. The marine was William Wedgeborough, the man who had fallen overboard off Eromanga, and now Cook must have wished that the man had managed to drown himself. Some kind of dispute had arisen but there seemed to be no need for the shooting and according to some reports Wedgeborough had shot the wrong man. Cook put him in irons, but luckily the islanders seemed to take the death very philosophically and the feared retribution against the visitors did not arise.

In spite of its small size, it was discovered that Tanna was inhabited by two separate races, one inhabiting the east and the other the west. The western islanders were in stature more like the Polynesian people of the Friendly Isles. At some time in the past they might have come from the east to make a settlement, but it was also possible that many generations ago their people had migrated to the east as the Melanesians arrived from the west and that they were a remnant who had stayed behind. Cook had landed amongst the Melanesian people of Tanna and the Polynesians were on the other side of the island. The two races cohabited on the same small island happily enough, but it seemed that their languages were quite different and that they were unable to understand each other. In spite of this problem, there must have been some communication and even marriage between two races living so closely together. William Wales spent a lot of time studying the Melanesian men throwing their spears and shooting arrows at various targets. His motive was to assess how lethal their weapons were. The men were very co-operative and willingly demonstrated their prowess. He concluded that they could throw as far as fifty yards but not with any accuracy. At a distance of about twenty yards, however, they could hit a man almost every time. He also noticed that they had a very graceful throwing action, which reminded him of Homer and the Greek classics.

Cook wanted to cut down a tree to make a new tiller for the ship. He was careful to obtain permission before the tree was felled. When the new tiller was fitted, he was ready to move on and the *Resolution* sailed back to the north, passing the western coasts of Eromanga, Efate and Malekula. His survey was incomplete: several islands had not been surveyed on their windward side. Even so, Cook's chart was still destined to serve as the best chart of the New Hebrides for a hundred years. He arrived at Espiritu Santo, which, although it was the largest island, did not seem to have a local name. He spent several days carefully circumnavigating and mapping and he made a brief landing. There was no sign of the Spanish colony, but this was not surprising given that it had existed for a very short period nearly two centuries previously. He identified Quiros's Bay of St Philip and St James on the north of the island; it was a harbour large enough to accommodate a thousand ships. He named the headland of the bay Cape Quiros. He also needed a name for the archipelago. The Hebrides was the nearest equivalent group in the British Isles. The hardy Scottish crofting community was very different from that of these tropical islands with their lush vegetation and active volcanoes, but nevertheless he decided to call the group the New Hebrides. Dr Johnson, whose tour of the Scottish Hebrides was undertaken in the previous year, was bound to approve of the name.

On the last day of August 1774 the ship headed off from the west end of the Bougainville Strait between Malekula and Espiritu Santo. The southern constellations filled the sky as they sailed to the south, leaving behind them a people untouched by modern civilisation. Across the silence of a moonlit Pacific night, they could hear the beating of the drums and the singing of the islanders with their ancient and undisturbed way of life. George Forster regretted that he did not have his friend James Burney with him. Of all the men on the *Adventure*, James was missed more than any, for he alone may have been able to take down and throw some light on the Melanesian music.

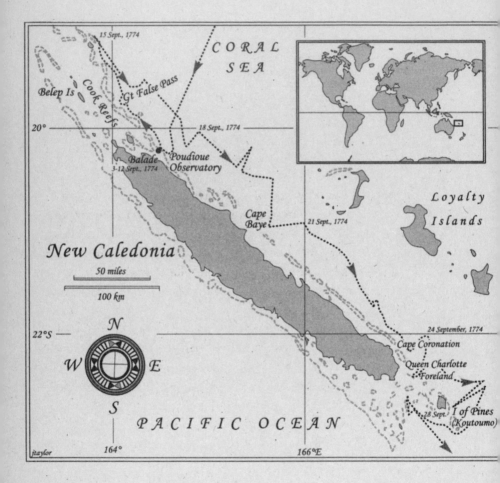

NINE

New Caledonia

And now the day had withdrawn from the sky, and Phoebe the
kindly moon was pounding half-Heaven with her night-wandering
chariot.

Aeneid, x, 215

Cook knew that he was only one or two days' sail from the Solomon
Islands, but he resisted the temptation to sail further to the north and
west. A rumour spread below decks that the *Resolution* was heading
home at last, but once again the men were quickly disappointed. The
captain had decided to head back to New Zealand and to search for
other islands on the way. For most of the voyage, Cook had been
following in the footsteps of previous explorers. Many of these
explorers, as we have seen, had crossed the Pacific one or even two
centuries earlier, and the current voyage, with modern instruments
and dietary knowledge, was a necessary tidying-up operation. Cook
had followed in the wake of vague sightings and descriptions, and
returned with full accounts, precise latitudes and longitudes, charts
and soundings for future navigators.

On leaving the New Hebrides, he could have been forgiven for
thinking that there was very little left to discover in this part of the
Pacific and that it would be a clear passage to the North Island of New
Zealand. But the Pacific was full of surprises and after only three days
at sea there was a cry of land. The first to see the land was a midshipman,
James Colnett, and, as was traditional, he was honoured by having the
headland named after him. They were approaching an extensive landfall
that stretched from the south-east to the north-west as far as the eye
could see. There were mountains streams and beaches guarded as usual
by treacherous coral reefs. It was another month before Cook knew the

full extent of the land he had discovered, but in fact it was nearly three hundred miles in length. It was exactly what James Cook always hoped and prayed for – a land even more virgin than the New Hebrides and with a people totally untouched by contact with other human civilisations.

The ship approached and canoes appeared to greet them. The ship came closer and the canoes retreated when they saw how large the invader was. There was great wonder and excitement on shore. The canoes came back again; they were double-hulled, with inverted triangular lateen sails and of a heavy construction, but they sailed fast and well. The twin hulls were joined by a wooden platform where the islanders could light a fire for cooking and the platform had holes so that the craft could be propelled with a paddle. The *Resolution* manœuvred to find a suitable anchorage inside the dangerous reef.

All this time the Natives to the number of 10 or 12 canoes lay on the two Points of the Reef seemingly wraped in astonishment at the address with which so large a body was turned and twisted about, and as soon as we were past them, they all up with their sails and followed us so that (to illustrate small things by large ones) we seemed like a Man-of-War, with a large fleet of Merchantmen under Convoy. We sailed thus between three & four Miles; the soundings being from 12 to 14 fathoms Clean Ground, and then came to the point of another Reef which extended South Eastward & seemed to Join the other about 5 or 6 miles higher up. Over the end of this we passed in 5 & 6 fathoms, having all the Way a Boat ahead sounding and Making signals. Within this reef lies a small sandy Island, under the Lee of which the Capt proposed to Anchor, and for that purpose made two or three boards to windward, the Natives following us all the time, tacking when we did and making signs of friendship, & satisfaction at our arrival.[1]

The reception committee was invited to come aboard. Then came a pleasant surprise after the experiences at the New Hebrides. The local people were shy and polite. They had weapons but they had no thoughts of using them and they readily exchanged clubs and spears for nails and red cloth. They were invited into the cabin and they inspected the contents of the ship. Above all, they did not pilfer and this alone was a unique, welcome and new experience on a Pacific Island. The ship was a great wonder to them, as were the pale-faced and red-faced men who sailed on her. But to see strange four-legged beasts – goats, pigs and dogs – running around on deck was an even greater novelty to them. The people had no large mammals on their island. The chief, whose name was Teabooma, invited the newcomers ashore. The clan gathered around and he made a short speech to which they all listened attentively. The name of the place, as far as they were able to discover from the inhabitants, was Balade.

A few days after their arrival, a partial eclipse of the sun took place. William Wales and Charles Clerke were anxious to observe it from the small sandy island they had passed on the way in. Cook was also a keen observer and he went to accompany them. The start of the eclipse was hidden by clouds, but they reached a good agreement – within a few seconds – on the end time and from this information Wales could calculate a precise longitude. The Forsters were also eager to go ashore but they were not given sufficient notice. Forster senior was convinced that the delay was deliberate and occasioned by jealousy on the part of the second lieutenant:

The Capt prepared to go to a little Isle, where the Astronomer was gone this morning, in order to observe there the Ecclipse. I desired the Capt to go ashore in the Afternoon, to collect more new things. We dined at one o'clock & when we just sat to our dinner the Officer sent & let me know the boats were going, because the Capt was absent. This was premeditated. They did not acquaint me they would go so early, nor could I go without dinner. In short the first Lieut wanted to disappoint me. He is a weak Man, & acts very inconsistent with himself & all principles of reason, & thought to do me a deal of harm by doing so, & after dinner he refused me a boat to let me go ashore, though there were hands enough to give me a cast to the very nigh shore, & many people were just then standing & laughing to divert the Indians: one traded before every bodies Eyes, another scratched a Sow to divert the Indians, but the Lieut said, he would break none off from their business: in short, the whole of the Affair is this, the greater part of the Men in the Ship have begun to calculate their pay & find that it will not amount to 4000£, Sterl., which government allows me. & therefore I am the object of their Envy & they hinder me in the pursuit of Natural History, where they can, from base & mean, dirty principles, beneath any Man of Sense. I get my Money if I had not the opportunity to get one plant or bird described the whole Voyage. If I am disappointed the fault is not mine, but the public looses by it, who pays & whose chief views are thus defeated, by Men who are Servants to the public, & ought to promote, not hinder the common cause. But it cannot be otherwise expected from the people who have not sense enough to think reasonably & beyond the Sphere of their mean grovelling Passions.[2]

Pickersgill took a boat with Gilbert, the ship's master, to the north-west, to explore the reef in the hope of finding a passage through. Cook, accompanied by native guides, took a party to climb to the top of the mountains. There, on the other side, they could see a large valley with a river meandering serpentine fashion, eventually reaching the sea on the far coast. They could see the other side of the island at a distance of about thirty miles. When he returned to the ship, Cook looked for Teabooma so that he could show his appreciation by giving a present, but the chief was nowhere to be found.

The islanders went around almost naked: the men wore a wrapper on the penis similar to the attire in the New Hebrides, and the women had short skirts or aprons. 'In short those People approach nearer to the Dress of Adam before he sewed the fig leaves together, than any we have seen before,' said William Wales. 'They are a handsome well-made People enough, and like all other naked people Active and nimble.' Their skin colour was dark copper, their hair jet black and frizzled – they seemed to be a cross between the Melanesian and Polynesian peoples. Cook could see some affinity with the aborigines of New South Wales but the language they spoke seemed to be Melanesian. They lived in round houses of about twenty feet diameter, similar in shape to a beehive, which had a kind of loft for storage. The upper floor was made from sticks woven crosswise and was used mainly for arms and utensils. The walls were made by driving posts into the ground with cross pieces at various heights and reeds set between them to a thick-ness of about four inches. The doorposts were decorated with carved heads, and the roofs were domed and thatched with reeds. They could make earthen pots from a fine red clay, a large example of which was boiling on their fire. William Wales paid them a great compliment for their honesty:

this country seems to be no Land of Canaan. However, if little can be said in Praise of the Country, much may be said of the goodness of its Inhabitants. Their honesty is the greatest I ever saw: and it is certainly from principle, for they are as fond of our things as any other people whatever: that of the Tanna People was supposed to proceed from their contempt, or rather dread of touching any thing we had, even when it was given to them for a few would take it otherwise than in a leaf, or some such thing. Nor is the Good-nature, Friendship or hospitality of these people a joy inferior to their Integrity: and Ill befall the Person who ever give them Cause to act otherwise.[3]

As the islanders bathed naked in the surf, a white man was spotted prancing around with them. The nudity that seemed natural to the Pacific islanders seemed offensive in a white man. Who was the man who had broken the ship's rules? He was not one of the sailors. He turned out to be one of the islanders, a rare case of an albino amongst the dark-skinned people.

Cook gave Teabooma a dog and a bitch. It was a present he had given at many islands previously but never before had the dogs been received with such obvious joy and appreciation. The chief could not believe his good fortune; he could hardly contain his joy at having two wonderful, lively, friendly and intelligent animals of his own. Cook took the trouble to record that the dog had a red and white coat; the bitch was also red, the colour of a fox. He called them the Adam and Eve of the island dog population. The bird population, in contrast to the mammals, was very numerous and Forster gives a colourful description of the tropical birds he saw there:

two fine green Parrots, with long tails & red on the Crown & Forehead, Wings & tail blue; the Neck yellow, Irides gold coloured, Feet & bill black, some had the tip of the bill yellow: on the crown were two narrow uprightstanding black Feathers, with red tips, of the length of the whole head. In short a quite new & beautifull bird. A yellowish Heron was shot with a black head, 3 white black tip'd long Feathers, Neck & breast pale rusty colour; Back, wings & tail red-chocolate colour, bill black. Feet greenish yellow. Lora naked greenish yellow. Irides yellow: but the bird stunk most immoderately.[4]

The Forsters were able to identify many new species, not only on land but also in the sea. A strange fish was caught with a large ugly head. It was a species they had never seen before and after George had made a drawing it was decided that it would make a good dinner. The fish turned out to be poisonous and several of the crew, including the captain, were taken ill after eating it. The ship's dogs, who had also eaten the fish were sick but they vomited up the fish and were soon fit again. One of the pigs, however, died from eating the entrails. It was an unfortunate incident but there were no serious consequences.

When the time came to move on, Cook made a formal claim to his new discovery. He found a large tree near the shore at the watering place and inscribed on it the name of King George, the name of his ship and other minor details. He knew that it was too risky to round the north cape of the island to reach the lee shore, and the *Resolution* therefore had to tack to the south and west and keep the reef at a safe distance. It was a dangerous coast to survey because of the treacherous reef and the very deep water that lay outside it. The lead line could seldom find a bottom even at two hundred fathoms. The prevailing winds tended to blow onshore, but this was better than a calm spell when the ship was entirely at the mercy of the treacherous tidal currents that could carry her on to the sharp coral. There were a few flat calms when the pinnace and the cutter had to be launched so that the ship could be towed laboriously by pulling on the oars. There was a small vessel of twenty tons' displacement stored in the hold which had been specially designed for this kind of dangerous survey work, but Cook decided against the effort of bringing it out of storage and putting it together. The small vessel consisted only of sawn timbers and had to be constructed practically from scratch, but most of the nails needed for its construction had been bartered for food and other items, Cook would therefore only have used it in an emergency. Progress was particularly dangerous during the dark nights, when it became impossible to judge distances and a careful eye had to be kept on the tides. Allowing for these problems, the survey went well. But the island was far longer than expected and there was no time to chart the lee coast.

At one point, as they were reaching the end of the land, some very strange objects were seen at a distance. They were tall pillars of some kind, but they were too far away to judge their height. Could these be the western Pacific equivalent of the great statues on Easter Island? As they sailed nearer, it was obvious that they were too tall to be man-made structures. They were either natural stone columns or unusual trees. Opinion on board the *Resolution* was divided as to which of the two, but Johann Forster thought his eyesight, supported by his spyglass, was better than that of everybody else on the ship. William Wales did not agree:

> The Shores, in most places, and all the low Land spoken of above exhibits a most extraordinary appearance, and seems as if it was full of exceeding high, upright, ragged Pillars of Wood or Stone; but which nevertheless I take to be Trees of a singular Nature: they are, if trees they be, certainly such as we have not seen before. One Gentleman in the True Spirit of the Ancient Philosophy Asserts & swears to it also that they are Pillars of Bizaltes [basalt] such as compose the Giants' Cawsway in Ireland & that he can see with his Glasses the Joints very distinctly, I have often been struck with Surprise at the Excellency of this Gentle-mans Eyes & Glasses or the Imperfection of My own. He has seen Oranges & Lemons Growing on ye trees at 3 Miles Distance & sworn positively to a Bird flying at upwards of one. I think it ought to be mentioned to the honour of Mr Ramsden that the Glass these feats have been done with was made by him, & is a common 2 feet Achromatic Spy-Glass.[5]

Cook thought they were trees. Forster thought they were basalt stone pillars. They made a wager of twelve bottles of wine, provided they could get close enough to prove the point one way or another. This involved some dangerous manœuvring, but once the wager had been made there was no going back and Cook took his ship inside the reef to investigate. As they came closer, the question of wood or stone could still not be settled. Opinion divided into two camps: the naval men thought them to be trees, the 'experimental' men, by which Forster presumably meant the scientific consort, went for rock pillars. In trying to reach the island, it was obvious that the ship had gone in far too close to the land and to return to the open sea was going to be a very arduous business. Cook tacked to the north and then back again to the south to try to get a good view of the breaking water, but there seemed to be shoals in all directions. The reef was about a mile to leeward and the soundings showed a bottom of fine sand. He felt that an anchor would not hold in the strong gale that was building up. Every available man was stationed around the ship, hanging on to the rigging with a rope in his hand and orders to yell out if he saw shoal water. There was a narrow escape when breakers appeared under the lee bow, but they managed to tack the ship and haul clear. Night fell but nobody was able to sleep because of the hidden danger that lay all around. When at last the dawn broke, it was to show that their fears were well founded: there was shallow water and breakers all around the ship. They took bearings on the headlands to calculate their position, only to find that they were in the same dangerous place as on the previous day and in spite of all their efforts they had gained nothing to windward during the night. It was a serious situation. Cook knew that he was in danger of losing his ship and with it the findings of the voyage and all his men. Perhaps the small vessel in the hold would have to be built after all. Others, too, were acutely aware of the dangers. William Wales recorded in his journal:

> We passed the Night standing too & from amongst these terrible Reefs expecting the ship to be brought up by some or other of them every Minute: to mend the Matter, it turned out exceeding dark, and I realy think our situation was to be envyed by very few except the Thief who has got the Halter about his Neck.[6]

Elliott's account was in complete agreement:

> In sailing round the Isle of Pines in the Evening, we found ourselves in a most dangerous situation, for the Man at the Mast Head called out: Breakers ahead. We hauled up several points, still Breakers ahead. In fact, we found that we had been running into a Net of Breakers (or Reef), and no way out, but as we had come in, which was now right in the Wind's Eye. The Winds increased as night came on, and every way we stood for an hour, the Roaring of the Breakers was heard. So that was a most anxious and perilous Night.[7]

When daylight appeared, they headed for the small island with the strange pillars. They dropped anchor near the mainland and took a boat to the island. As they got closer, some of the stone party defected to trees, but Johann Forster stubbornly held out until they were very close and branches covered with a thin green foliage became visible. They had discovered a species of spruce pine that had never been encountered before; it consisted of a solid trunk growing to about seventy feet but with a span of only about six feet. The ship's carpenter declared the wood to be excellent for the ship's spars: he declared that with the possible exception of the North Island of New Zealand, they were the best ship's timbers in the Pacific. The point had been settled and Cook had won his wager, but there remained the problem of getting the ship back to the open sea. Again it was a very close thing:

> We sailed again on the 30th, and in going out, had it not been for the intervention of providence, a good look out, and quick working, we must still have been lost, for the Breakers were seen close under our Bows, when the Ship was thrown instantly about, and by that means saved, and proceeded to Sea. Leaving the other side of the Country unexplored, but we saw enough of it to be certain it was not more than 30 Miles broad.[8]

They thankfully cleared the reef and went out into the open sea. Cook, having already honoured Scotland by naming the previous island group the New Hebrides, conferred a double honour by giving his latest discovery the name of New Caledonia. His father, whom he had seen for a few days on his visit to Yorkshire, was a Scot, which doubtless made him conscious of his Scottish ancestry and it may have been a contributory factor.

At last the *Resolution* was heading south to New Zealand. There was one minor discovery on the way: this was a small uninhabited island whose most vociferous residents were the birds. In spite of its small size, the island had a fresh water supply and a rare plant species that they named a cabbage tree. The cabbage grew at the crown of the tree and proved very palatable compared to the shipboard food. It was rumoured that the Duchess of Norfolk had requested that an Island be named after her and for this reason Cook called it Norfolk Island. They were soon sailing south again and on 17 October a snow-capped peak appeared on the horizon. It was easily identified as Mount Egmont on the north coast of New Zealand. The *Resolution* tacked to the west and sailed right into a thunderstorm; the heavy seas split the jib sail into pieces. The ship was badly in need of an overhaul, but Cook had sailed this way before; he knew the coast well and there was little danger. The *Resolution* rounded Cape Everard and entered Queen Charlotte Sound. Soon she was anchored at Ship Cove for the third time on the voyage.

The first thing the captain did was to look for the message in the bottle. The bottle had gone. This did not prove the *Adventure* had been there: anybody could have taken the message. Then William Wales, as he was setting up his observatory, noted that several trees that had been standing on the last visit had been felled with axe and saw. This seemed to be conclusive proof that the *Adventure* had been at Ship Cove and had received the message that Cook had left for her.

On one of the islands they saw a pig which they had left behind and which seemed to be fending well for itself without the help of the Maoris. A sow was taken from the ship to join it, only to find that what they took for a boar was actually a sow! The Maoris arrived and they were keen enough to trade, but only a few faces were recognised from the last visit of almost a year ago. Cook began to make enquiries about the *Adventure*, only to find that he received strange and mixed emotions, with evasive and inconsistent answers to his questions. Yes, the ship had been, but the Maoris claimed to know nothing of the welfare of the crew. It became obvious that they were hiding something since all the stories were different. Then a horrific story was told that the *Adventure* had been wrecked on the far shore and that their enemies on the North Island had killed and eaten the crew. Cook did not take the story seriously enough to send an expedition to search for the wreckage. The Maoris who were directly involved in the massacre of Grass Cove took great pains to stay well away from the *Resolution*, so that all the crew heard was hearsay and second-hand. The language barrier made it difficult to communicate. Cook knew that something untoward had happened, but he did not discover the truth. Even if he had discovered Grass Cove, where the massacre had taken place, the evidence he needed was no longer there.

By this time, William Wales had made many calculations of the longitude of Queen Charlotte Sound. On the previous visits he had implied that Cook's chart from the *Endeavour* had been laid down about eighty nautical miles to the east. At first, Cook did not believe that the error could be so great – the longitudes on his previous voyage had been calculated by the lunar methods and they were verified by an observation of the transit of Mercury by Charles Green, the *Endeavour* astronomer. Cook had every faith in Charles Green, but now that he had become well acquainted with William Wales he had seen how carefully and seriously Wales took his work. Any single longitude calculation could be in error by as much as forty minutes, but not the mean of the dozens of observations that Wales had taken. Cook finally had to accept that his carefully made chart was in error; in fact, the error was only about half what Wales calculated, but this still hurt his pride. Even Wales, with the help of Kendall's chronometer, was half a degree out in his calculations. Although the problem of finding the longitude was effectively solved, the errors were still of the order of about twenty nautical miles and more than this if only a single observation was available. The watch could measure small differences in longitude very accurately, but on a long voyage of many months the error accumulated.

I mention these errors not from a supposition that they will much effect either Navigation or Geography, but because I have no doubt of their existence, for from the multitude of observations which Mr Wales took the situation of few parts of the world are better assertained than that of Queen Charlottes Sound. Indeed I might with equal truth say the same of all the other places where we have made any stay at. For Mr Wales, whose abilities is equal to his assiduity, lost no one observation that could possibly be obtained. Even the situation of such Islands as we past without touching at are by means of Mr Kendalls Watch determined with almost equal accuracy. The Error of the Watch from Otaheite to this place was only $43'39\frac{1}{4}''$ In Longitude reckoning at the rate it was found to go at that Island and at Tanna. But by reckoning at the rate it was going when last at this place and from the time of our leaving it to our return to it again which was near a year the error was $19°31'35''$ in time, or $4°52'48\frac{3}{4}''$ in Longitude. This error can not be thought great if we consider the length of time and that we had gone over a space equal to upwards of three quarters of the Equatorial Circumference of the Earth and through all the Climates and Latitudes

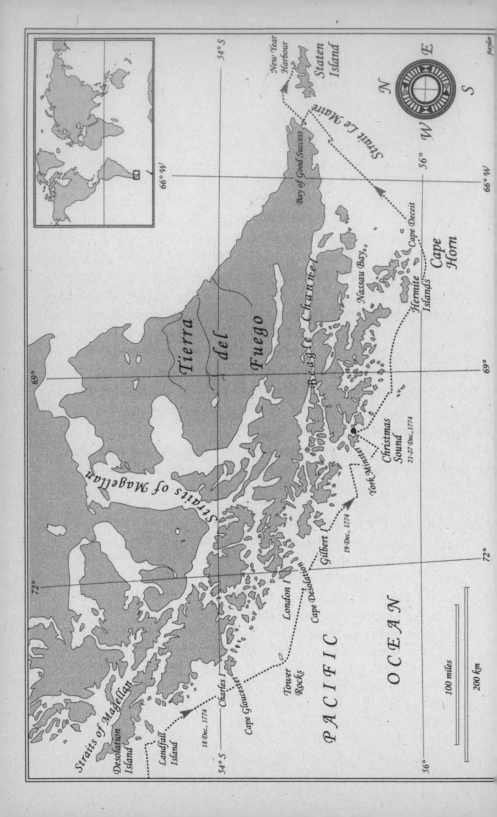

from 9° to 71°. Mr Wales found its true rate of going here to be that of gaining 12" 576 on mean time per day. The Mean Result of all the observations which he made for assertaining the Variation of the Compass and the dip of the south end of the Needle the three several times we have been here gave $14°09\frac{1}{5}'$ East for the former and $64°36\frac{2}{3}'$ for the latter.[9]

There were a few minor incidents at Ship Cove. John Marra, who had tried to desert the ship at Tahiti, made a second attempt in New Zealand. Cook would not have been sorry to be rid of him: he was tempted to turn a blind eye and let him stay to make his way with the Maoris, but Marra returned of his own accord. On 11 November 1774 the *Resolution* left New Zealand to make a direct passage to Cape Horn. It was an emotional farewell to a land they had come to know and love and which had provided the base for the exploration of the Antarctic and the South Pacific. With her mainsail filled by the breeze, the *Resolution* cleared Cape Koamaroo and the view from the deck showed the entrance to Queen Charlotte Sound. They passed the now familiar but deserted Maori hippa at the end of the promontory. It was a fine morning, visibility was good and on the horizon the mountains around them could be clearly seen, their summits covered with snow. They navigated the choppy waters of Cook Straits but as they came under Cape Campbell they were sheltered from the wind and the ship slowed down. The neighbouring hills seemed to have white chalky spots with traces of marl and beyond lay a good tract of low fertile land. Cloudy Bay did not live up to its name. As they sailed by, they could see clearly right into the large, spacious and deep bay. The mountains beyond were surrounded by layers of mist but their snow-covered peaks could be seen above the clouds. In the wake of the *Resolution* came shrieking black shearwaters, followed by diving petrels, a Port Egmont hen and a graceful albatross. The ship cleared the Cook Straits for the last time, rounded Cape Palliser and set her sails for the east and the long voyage to Cape Horn.

The *Resolution* made a fast passage across the Pacific at a latitude of about 50°, intersecting the previous year's route in three places and covering a lot of previously unexplored ocean but without finding even the smallest speck of land. This was no great surprise to Cook: he was fully convinced that there could be no major landmass in this part of

the Pacific. It took only twenty-seven days to get from New Zealand
to the western exit from the Straits of Magellan. Here, where every
other captain would have stood well out to sea to clear Cape Horn,
Cook made straight for the treacherous and forbidding south coast of
Tierra del Fuego. This, the southernmost part of the Americas, was a
formidable iron-bound coast, a coastline made up of broken cliffs,
fjords and many small islands. The ship's master, Joseph Gilbert, was
honoured with an island named after him:

> in this situation we were about 3 leagues from the nearest shore which
> was that of an island which I named Gilbert Isle after my Master. It is
> near of equal height with the rest of the Coast and shews a surface
> composed of several peaked rocks of unequal height. A little to the SE
> of it were some smaller Islands and without them breakers. I have before
> observed that this is the most desolate coast I ever saw, it seems to be
> intirely composed of Rocky Mountains without the least appearence of
> Vegetation, these Mountains terminate in horroable precipices whose
> craggy summits spire up to a vast hieght, so that hardly any thing in
> nature can appear with a more barren and savage aspect than the whole
> of this coast. The inland mountains were covered with Snow but those
> on the Sea Coast were not; we judged the former to belong to the Main
> of Terra del Fuego and the latter to be islands so ranged as apparently
> to form a Coast.[10]

The coast had never before been seen at such close quarters and the
names that Cook gave to the capes, rocks, bays and islands reflected
the nature of the barren coast. First there was Landfall Island, then
Tower Rocks, Fury Island, Cape Desolation, Burnt Island, Great Black
Rocks, Little Black Rocks and then Desolation Island. Tower Rocks
stood high out of the sea. York Minster was a similar formation, which
bore only the slightest resemblance to its namesake. A few features were
named after places, for example London Island and Cape Gloucester.
Christmas Sound and Goose Island commemorated two closely linked
events on the voyage. The island was occupied by a large colony of
geese, who very understandably moved off as the sailors moved in, but
the crew was still able to procure sixty-two of them, so that goose
formed the basis of the main course of the next day's meal, which
happened to be the third Christmas Day of the voyage. There were

enough geese for one bird to be shared between three seamen. There was still plenty of liquor on board and the party lasted two days until Cook decided to put the drunkards ashore to sober up.

Nearby he named Waterman Island, Cook Bay and Philip Rocks. He did not know it, but there was actually a channel through to the Atlantic here that cut off part of Tierra del Fuego. The passage was discovered more than fifty years later and became known as the Beagle Channel when Robert Fitzroy's ship of that name explored this same coast. In fact, the coast was so little visited that the *Beagle* was the next ship after the *Resolution* to explore the south coast of Tierra del Fuego. Fitzroy carried a young naturalist called Charles Darwin on board and this was the reason why his voyage became even more famous than that of the *Resolution*.

Tierra del Fuego was given its name, 'land of the fires', early in the sixteenth century by Ferdinand Magellan, the first European explorer to enter the Pacific Ocean. The fires were lit by the native Fuegians who inhabited the land. It was a cold and miserable country with few natural resources. It was surprising that any race could survive the cold winter and find enough fuel to keep warm and sufficient food to stay alive. Yet the Fuegians were quite numerous and they were spread throughout the main island. They came to visit the ship at Christmas Sound; four canoes came to trade. The visitors had hard features, broad faces, prominent cheekbones, flat nostrils and large mouths: their straight black hair was covered in thrane oil, and hung dank and untended around their face. They covered their bodies with the same oil, partly to keep warm. Their language seemed to consist of grunts and lisps. The explorers thought them the most miserable people on earth and the Fuegians stank so much that the sailors claimed to smell them a hundred paces downwind. Cook did not go through the nose-rubbing ceremony and they were not invited to Christmas dinner.

Another who did not enjoy the Christmas dinner was the marine William Wedgeborough. He fell overboard for the second time on the voyage. His accident was not witnessed and he drowned in the icy waters. Another man who nearly drowned was young Elliott. He tells an amazing story of how, on his seventeenth birthday, he rambled ashore with his messmate Roberts to try to shoot a goose. He shot and wounded a bird, but it was still able to fly, took wing out to sea for about fifty yards and then fell into the water. Sea lions swam out and nosed around it. Then two marines arrived and Elliott offered a bottle of rum to either of them to swim out and retrieve his goose; he offered to cover them with a gun if the sea lions came near. The marines laughed at him and refused to risk their lives in such a foolhardy stunt. After some hesitation, Elliott stripped off and plunged into the freezing waters off Cape Horn and swam out amidst the sea lions to retrieve his goose. He got back alive, but he admitted that it was the most stupid and dangerous exploit of his life.

The ship arrived at False Cape Horn, with the true Cape Horn, the southernmost point on the Americas, about twelve leagues to the south-east. She rounded perilously close to the world's most notorious cape and headed north-east into the Straits Le Maire. She passed through with ease, and Cook noted the Bay of Good Success, where he had landed with the *Endeavour* five years ago. He still held a faint hope that the *Adventure* might have remained to explore the Pacific and that she might still be behind them, so he left a message at the bay for Captain Furneaux. The *Resolution* passed through the straits with Staten Island on the starboard. Here, they were treated to a mating display by the largest creatures on earth.

a Whale of about 30 or 40 foot long turned on its back & kept the belly uppermost & began to beat on both Sides the Sea with a terrible blow with his long Pectoral fins, which as well as the tail are black above & white below, the belly seemed to have longitudinal wrinkles. Sometimes the Whale fairly jumped out of the Water with the whole body & fell again into it with a loud Explosion made by his Fins: nor is this Astonishing that a huge mass of about 40 or more feet long & 8 or 10 feet diameter should cause a great Explosion by its heavy fall into the Water. Sometimes there were two Whales frisking together in this manner, & certainly the greater part of the Whales we saw were all in couples, probably this is their time for Love, & this tumbling of these huge Masses are only the Preludes precedent to it . . .[11]

It was New Year's Day 1775. The eighteenth century had entered its last, revolutionary quarter. The *Resolution* was no longer in the

Pacific Ocean but back again in the Atlantic. Was Captain Cook going to take the direct route northwards and home along the coast of South America? No. The work of this incredible voyage was still unfinished.

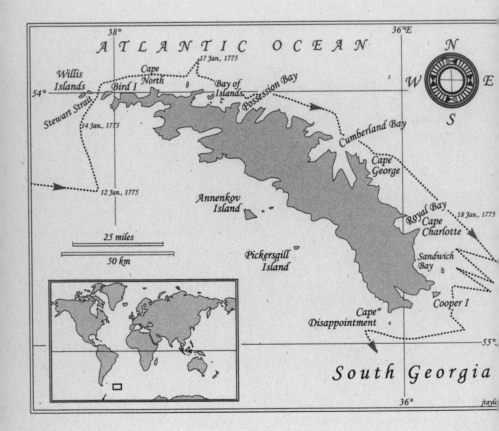

ATLANTIC OCEAN

Willis
Islands
54°
Stewart Strait

Cape
North
Bird I

38°

17 Jan., 1775

Bay of
Islands

Possession Bay

Cumberland Bay

36°E

N
W   E
S

14 Jan., 1775

12 Jan., 1775

25 miles

50 km

Annenkov
Island

Pickersgill
Island

Cape
George

Royal Bay   18 Jan., 1775
Cape
Charlotte

Sandwich
Bay

Cooper I

55°

Cape
Disappointment

South Georgia

36°

jtaylo

TEN

The Atlantic

All were of the same opinion, to quit the accursed land, to leave a
place where hospitality was defiled and give over our ship to the
south winds.

Aeneid, III, 60, 61

According to Dalrymple's *Voyages*, land had been sighted at some distance to the east of Cape Horn, but exactly at what distance and in which precise direction was rather a moot point. In 1675 a London merchant, Antoine de la Roch, discovered 'a large and pleasant island' somewhere in the vicinity, a description that appears to be a very inaccurate sighting of the Falkland Islands. In 1765 the Frenchman Ducloz Guyot in his ship the *Leon* was carried many leagues off course after rounding Cape Horn and he sighted an island of icy cliffs in the South Atlantic. The positions for both sightings were erroneous, but Cook decided it was still worthwhile to explore the area around them.

The *Resolution* headed to the south-east and on 14 January the Welshman Thomas Willis sighted a small rocky island that Cook decided to name after him. Behind were other small islands, but then came a great mass of land rising high out of the sea; it was worthy of investigation, with sea passages to both north and south. Cook chose to explore the northern coast first. The land turned out to be a barren coast with tall cliffs of ice rising sheer from the sea to the clouds. It was a frozen wintry landscape, too cold for running water and too cold to support any vegetation. Had they stumbled upon the desolate coast of the Antarctic continent? Wherever it was, it proved that Tierra del Fuego was not, after all, the most depressing and isolated place on the face of the earth. Cook's journal described the latest find as he witnessed the icebergs being born:

The head of the Bay, as well as two places on each side, was terminated by a huge Mass of Snow and ice of vast extent, it shewed a perpendicular cliff of considerable height, just like the side or face of an ice isle; pieces were continually breaking from them and floating out to sea. A great fall happened while we were in the Bay; it made a noise like a cannon. The inner parts of the country was not less savage and horrible: the Wild rocks raised their lofty summits till they were lost in the Clouds and the Vallies laid buried in everlasting snow. Not a tree or shrub was to be seen, no not seen big enough to make a toothpick . . .[1]

'I did not think it worth my while to go and examine these places where it did not seem probable that any one would ever be benefited by the discovery,' he added. He kept his ship well offshore: the horror of a shipwreck on such a coast was unthinkable. He chose to land in one of the boats and formally took possession at a place he called Possession Bay; he hoisted the flag and fired three volleys which frightened the seals and penguins and echoed eerily from the barren icy cliffs. He decided to name the land after King George and it became known as South Georgia. Capes were named after King George and Queen Charlotte, and Saunders Bay was named after Admiral Charles Saunders. An island was named Cooper Island after the first lieutenant and another named Pickersgill Island after the third lieutenant. Then, at the extreme south of the land, came Cape Disappointment from where they could see the south coast of the new discovery. It was obvious that the land was exactly what they had suspected all the time: only an island and not part of a continent.

Cook continued to sail in a south-easterly direction and soon they were making new discoveries again. Bare icy headlands and barren peaks added depression and mixed emotions to the excitement of the new discoveries. The first island, named Thule Island, turned out to be the furthest south of an archipelago. Then came a barren rocky island named Freezeland, a very appropriate name but named after able-bodied seaman Samuel Freezeland, who first spotted it. Nearby was Cape Bristol, rising high and icy from the sea, with a deep bay named Forster Bay to the south; it was the first feature to be named after the ship's naturalist since Forster Lake at Dusky Sound. Both names lasted only a very short time since it was soon realised that the features were isolated islands and not part of a continuous coastline.

Forster's Bay became Forster's Passage that ran between Bristol Island and Thule Island to the south. Then came Montague Island, Saunders Island and Candlemas Island. Cook called the group the Sandwich Islands after the First Lord of the Admiralty. Lieutenant Clerke summarised the general feelings about the new discoveries:

> What we've hitherto seen of this Land is I believe as wretched a Country as Nature can possibly form – the shores are formed of rocky and Icy Cliffs and precipices – we've not yet seen a Hole we cou'd shove a Boat in, much less the Ship; we here and there see Points of Land which must doubtless form Bays etc but the intermediate spaces are quite choked up with Ice, which breaks off in perpendicular Cliffs into the sea as high as the adjacent shores; at some short intervals when the Haze clears a little, we see mountains of immense bulk and height a distance in Land, but totally cover'd with Snow as is the whole face of the Country throughout.[2]

Cook again witnessed the icebergs being formed in the same way as they had broken off from the cliffs of South Georgia. The Antarctic seas were full of these floating ice islands and this left him in no doubt that there was a terrible and inhospitable land to the south where Nature was creating the bulk of the icebergs. The land was so far to the south that it was inaccessible to man. He gave his views on Antarctica:

> The risk one runs in exploring a coast in these unknown and Icy Seas, is so very great, that I can be bold to say, that no man will ever venture farther than I have done and that the lands which may lie to the South will never be explored. Thick fogs, Snow storms, Intense Cold and every other thing that can render Navigation dangerous one has to encounter and these difficulties are greatly heightned by the enexpressable horrid aspect of the Country, a Country doomed by Nature never once to feel the warmth of the Suns rays, but to lie for ever buried under everlasting snow and ice. The Ports which may be on the Coast are in a manner wholy filled up with frozen Snow of a vast thickness, but if any should so far be open as to admit a ship in, it is even dangerous to go in, for she runs a risk of being fixed there for ever, or coming out in an ice island. The islands and floats of ice on the Coast, the great falls from the ice clifts in the Port, or a heavy snow storm attended with a sharp frost, would prove equally fatal. After such an explanation as this the reader

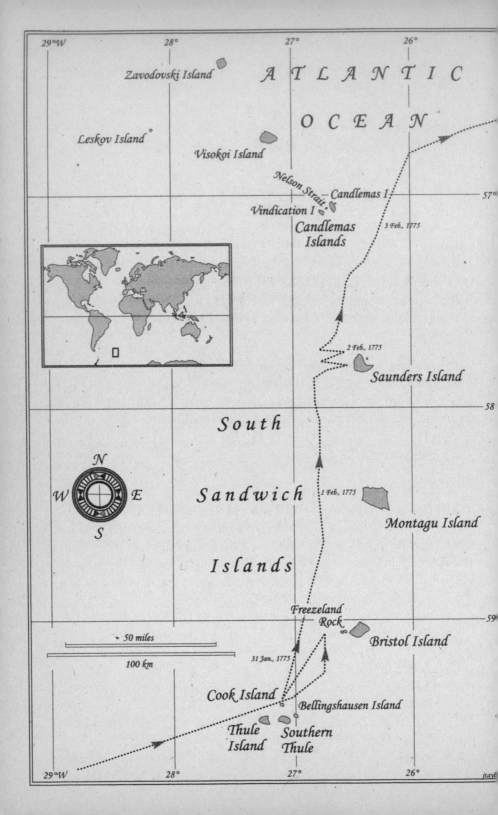

must not expect to find me much farther to the South. It is however not for want of inclination but other reasons. It would have been rashness in me to have risked all which had been done in the Voyage, in finding out and exploaring a Coast which when done would have answerd no end whatever, or been of the least use either to Navigation or Geography or indeed any other Science . . .[3]

Cook decided to head north again in the hope of finding the elusive Cape Circumcision which he had been unable to find when he left Cape Town over two years before. The ship sailed east at a latitude of 58° but they still could not find Bouvet's elusive cape. The long voyage and the protracted cold were affecting everybody and even James Cook was feeling the strain. Forster senior became more irritable than ever and at one point Cook had to throw him out of his cabin. A dispute flared up amidships between Willis, Loggie, Coglan, Price and Maxwell – these five were always at loggerheads with each other and Cook called them his 'black sheep'. Loggie was normally a good-tempered young man but he had drunk too much and he became very belligerent when he was the worse for drink. After one of the drunken bouts, Cook put Loggie in irons on the quarterdeck to sober him up but Loggie hurled abuse at the captain. At one point, Loggie and Coglan drew their knives on the ship's cook; then a squabble developed between Loggie and Maxwell which reached a crisis when Loggie drew his knife on Maxwell and attempted to stab him. Maxwell complained to the captain and showed the scratch made by the knife as he tried to defend himself. Cook believed Maxwell's account of the incident and ordered Loggie to the gangway and had him flogged like a common sailor. But the crew knew the personalities involved: they pitied Loggie and turned against Maxwell. Cook, too, regretted his action. It was a rare lapse of judgement. In spite of suffering the verbal abuse, he restored Loggie to his post and treated him with more consideration. After this breach of discipline, Cook read the articles of war to the crew. There were other problems besides the intense cold. The last barrel of sauerkraut was opened – the ship had started the voyage with eighty barrels. The food was monotonous, salty and unhealthy, and now that the sauerkraut had been finished it was inevitable that scurvy would set in. It was time to make for the aptly named Cape of Good Hope.

On 16 March they saw a sail – in fact, they saw two sets of sails. They belonged to two Dutch vessels. This was a moving moment on the voyage, for, with the exception of her consort the *Adventure*, the Dutch vessels were the first ships the *Resolution* had seen since leaving Cape Town thirty moons ago. Would the Dutch know who they were and would they know anything of the fate of the *Adventure*? What had been happening in the world since they departed from the Cape of Good Hope? Cook took the precaution of collecting in all the journals and papers that the crew had kept on the journey. He wanted to come alongside the Dutch and the next day he was able to send a boat across for news. When they heard his story, the Dutch gave him sugar and other supplies. The latest venture of Captain Cook was well known in Cape Town. The Dutch were eager to exchange news and they told him that the *Adventure* had anchored safely at the Cape a year ago. They also told him the bad news: the story of the sailors who had been killed and eaten by the cannibals in New Zealand. Cook was badly shaken; he had made many friends amongst the Maoris and his first reaction was one of disbelief. The next day, another ship was sighted, flying the British colours. She was the *True Briton*, homeward bound from China, and she confirmed that the story told by the Dutch was correct. It left Cook in a dilemma. He had come to know the Maori culture better than any other man alive, yet he was now forced to accept that the rumours he had heard at Ship Cove were based on the truth – his own men had been murdered and cannibalised.

The *True Briton* did not intend to put in at Cape Town, so Cook sent a brief report with her to the Admiralty. This news, that the *Resolution* was within two days' sail of Cape Town, was the first that the waiting friends and relatives heard at home. The next day, the Cape of Good Hope was sighted and in the night there was a very unusual sight – a rainbow created by the light of the moon. Their search had taken them to the east beyond the longitude of the Cape and they now followed the coast to the west, tacking against the prevailing winds. The Cape was rounded and the following day Table Mountain was visible at about ten leagues to the north-east. They landed on Wednesday 22 March to find that the day was Tuesday 21 in Cape Town, a reminder that they had sailed around the world and that their dates had not been corrected since the day they sailed from the same port two and a half years ago. They had crossed the 180° meridian five times and Cook calculated that the ship had sailed twenty thousand leagues, well over twice the distance around the Equator.

It was a strange experience to be back again in the civilised world when they had seen no European company except their own for so long. There was news of the war in the Middle East and the English newspapers reported the unrest in the American Colonies. There was good company, with wholesome Dutch hospitality, delicious fresh food after the months at sea, green vegetables and the luxury of wines and freshly baked bread. Cook found lodgings ashore. He allowed the men shore leave and was amused to see his sea-legged sailors clumsily riding on horseback. He was fortunate to meet the Frenchman Captain Julian Crozet who was second in command to Marion du Fresne in the *Mascarin*, the ship that narrowly beat the *Adventure* to Tasmania. Both captains enjoyed comparing notes of their discoveries.

There was a letter from Tobias Furneaux which described the terrible massacre at Grass Cove and the reasons why he had decided not to remain in the Pacific. It was at Cape Town that Cook first saw Hawkesworth's account of the *Endeavour* voyage. He was not happy with it   the introduction claimed that he himself had checked the contents when he knew perfectly well that he had been on the other side of the world and had done no such thing. It had in fact been checked by Joseph Banks, but some of Banks's quotations were accounted to Cook and vice versa. The book was an abbreviated account because it covered the circumnavigations of both Byron and Wallis as well as Cook. It was unfortunate, however, that Cook took a dislike to Hawkesworth's account since the book was actually very accurate in many important details. It was well illustrated with high-quality woodcuts and was a very fine example of the eighteenth-century bookmaker's craft. It was widely read at the time and it did Cook's reputation no harm at all, but the fact that he disowned the account meant that his biographers tended to ignore Hawkesworth. In the long term, it was of little consequence for the original story was retained intact by the journals of Cook and Banks and those who sailed on the voyage.

Cook stayed only the minimum time in Cape Town. The sails and rigging of the *Resolution* were in a terrible state and the tiller had to be detached from the ship for repairs. She needed a thorough re-caulking but otherwise she had come through the ordeal in good shape. The irony was that after travelling around the world without losing a boat, two of the ship's boats were lost at Cape Town. The cutter, which was moored alongside the ship, simply decided to sink, losing masts, sails and oars in the process. The jolly boat broke away from her moorings, was driven out to sea and was never found again. If this had happened in the Pacific, it would have created a serious problem, but luckily there was no problem about finding replacement boats.

'After taking leave of all our friends, and particularly of Dr Sparrman, who had shared the perils and distresses of our voyage, and whose heart had endeared him to all who knew him, we came on board on the twenty-seventh in the morning,' wrote George Forster. Anders Sparrman decided to stay at Cape Town for another year. He sailed with the ship as far as Robben Island and then said his farewells and took a boat back to Cape Town. The *Resolution* left Cape Town in company with a Danish Indiaman, a Spanish frigate and a British East Indiaman, the *Dutton* under Captain Henry Rice. The achievements of Cook and the *Resolution* were known and appreciated by both the Danish and Spanish. They fired salutes of thirteen guns, which the British returned. There was music from the deck of the Danish ship as she sailed alongside the *Resolution*; it was a compliment to Captain Cook. Spirits were high and Cook resolved to take a direct line to St Helena. When Captain Rice suggested he might miss the island, Cook laughed and showed his rare sense of humour, claiming that he could run his jib sail into the island. 'It would not be doing justice to Mr Harrison and Mr Kendall if I did not own that we have received very great assistance from this useful and valuable time piece as will more fully appear in the course of this Journal,' he wrote. He was confident that with the help of the chronometer his navigation was perfect enough to get within a few miles of any point on the surface of the globe. The longitude of St Helena was very well known and it had a very respectable astronomical history. The young Edmund Halley was there for two years in the 1670s, cataloguing the stars of the southern hemisphere; the current Astronomer Royal, Neville Maskelyne, had observed from St Helena in 1769; Mason and Dixon had also been able to establish the longitude. The position was known as accurately as any place on earth.

The stop at St Helena gave the crew another relaxed interlude, but

Cook could not understand why wheeled vehicles were deliberately parked outside his window. On enquiry, he found that Hawkesworth's published account of his earlier voyage stated that there were no wheeled vehicles on the island and the residents were anxious to make the point that Hawkesworth was wrong. The other objection they raised was the mention of slave labour. This was a sensitive issue, considering that all the vineyards were worked by slaves. The movement for the abolition of the slave trade was well under way and it was a very controversial topic.

The governor of the island was John Skottowe, who was married to a local girl. This was particularly pleasing to James Cook, for Skottowe hailed from his own birthplace of Great Ayton in the North Riding of Yorkshire. In fact, when James Cook was a boy, his father had been foreman to Skottowe's father and Cook himself well remembered helping on the farm. Unlike the Cooks, the Skottowes were of the gentry and James Cook had every reason to be grateful to Thomas Skottowe, father of the governor, for his early education. Thomas Skottowe was one of the enlightened members of the local gentry; he recognised that young James Cook had potential and had paid the small fees for him to attend the Postgate School at Ayton. It was therefore very rewarding for the governor of St Helena to see his father's investment so well rewarded. The community at St Helena was always glad to entertain visitors and in the evening they threw a ball at which Forster picked out Mrs Skottowe as the sprightliest lady on the island.

> We returned in the Evening & after dressing we went to the Governor's House, where Mr Graham gave a ball to the Ladies of the Place, to which we were likewise invited. The assembly was numerous & brilliant by the really great number of fine women, Natives of this happy Isle, whose fair Complexion, fine Shape and features & agreeable easy lively manners, & ready parts makes them equal to the fairs ones of any country.

The proceedings lasted until three in the morning.

It was with regrets that the convoy left St Helena and sailed for Ascension Island. Here, the merchantmen had to part company because they had strict instructions from their employers not to call at Ascension Island. The reason was because of smuggling operations. The

Americans sailed their small boats right across the Atlantic to try to purchase spices from the east without paying the customs. The *Resolution* also parted company with the *Dutton*, but Cook sent his valuable reports with Captain Rice under the capable charge of Isaac Smith. At Ascension Island they gathered a collection of timber from a large wrecked ship, which seemed to have caught fire and subsequently had been beached by its crew who had then abandoned it. The timber was of little value except as fuel, but the *Resolution* was running short and was therefore glad of it. They were also able to stock up on turtle meat: the crew of a previous ship had left the turtles on the beach, suffering and lying helplessly on their backs. It was a pointless piece of cruelty which upset both Cook and the Forsters.

Cook then made a very characteristic decision. He made up his mind to sail his ship one thousand miles to the west where the island of Fernando de Noronha lay off the coast of Brazil. It would mean an extra two weeks on the journey and his only reason for this detour across the Atlantic was so that he could measure the longitude of the island that he knew had never been ascertained before. The island was found with very little trouble, the only problem being that the short-sighted midshipman on the look-out could not see it when all on deck could see it clearly. It had a peaked mountain so steep that it looked like a church spire and there were two castles, with the Portuguese flag flying from one of them. In addition to the castles, there were no less than five forts. The Portuguese certainly intended to defend the island against invasion, but Cook reasoned that it would not be difficult to starve them out. Cook saluted as his ship sailed around the island. He had measured the correct longitude and did not consider it worthwhile to make a landing. The puzzled Portuguese saw a crazy English ship approach their island and immediately head off to the north without even attempting to land.

The Atlantic tour was beginning to bear some resemblance to the previous year in the Pacific. The *Resolution* crossed the Equator at last, then headed northwards to the Azores and docked at the port of Fayal on 14 July. Here they heard news of the problems in the American colonies, and reports of the battle at Bunker Hill came from an American vessel. The stay at the island lasted five days. Supplies were plentiful and abundant, but the English were unable to enter into society

gatherings as had been possible at St Helena. The Azores was a very
religious community and Johann Forster visited one of the three
churches in Fayal:

> There are three Parish-Churches in Town: the principal of which is
> called *Matriz* & stands on the North Side of the Town. another Parish
> is quite on its northernmost Extremity: & the third is beyond the Fort
> to the South near *Porto Pim* & is called *Nossa Senhora da Angustias*. The
> Churches have allmost all the same Structure & ornaments viz: a great
> Altar opposite the Entrance at the bottom of the Church. & two smaller
> Altars on each Side. A gallery opposite the Great Altar, & commonly 2
> Pulpits one opposite to another, where two Preachers at a time, as I was
> told, undertake in one the Cause of God Almighty, & that of the Host
> of Angels & Saints, & in the other that of Lucifer & his host & the
> poor Devil is certainly to be fairly beaten every time. The Altars are
> sculptured & ornamented with a great Deal of trifling tinsel: some are
> made of Cedar-wood & perfume the whole Church with the Fragrancy
> of the wood.[5]

There were several monasteries, consisting of Franciscan, Carmelite
and Capuchin monks, but the Forsters, who were looking for a cultural
contact, found the monks very ignorant of current affairs and scientific
matters. The elder Forster complained that one of the monks tried to
sell him a pipe of wine. His son George thought they led a completely
idle and ignorant life and he attributed the cause to the Prime Minister
of Portugal, who prohibited the printing of any kind of gazette or
newspaper. They met only one priest who knew any Latin; he had
published an article in a Spanish political and learned journal.

George Forster and some of his companions were introduced to a
widow in Fayal, a Mrs Milton, who had settled there. When she heard
who they were and from where they had travelled, she suddenly burst
into a flood of tears and lamentations. It transpired that her son William
Milton, a boy of nineteen when he left home, had sailed on the *Adventure* – he was one of the seamen murdered at Grass Cove. Reflecting
on the manner of his horrible death and other misfortunes that had
embittered her life, Mrs Milton had decided to confine her fourteen-
year-old daughter inside the cloisters of one of the convents of Fayal.
One of the naval officers, fired up with zeal to save a beautiful girl from
what he thought was a cruel sacrifice, expostulated with the mother

when he heard this news, saying that far from gaining heaven the girl would bring upon herself eternal displeasure. 'I leave the reader to determine whether a seaman's admonition could have much effect,' said George Forster. 'Mrs Milton, however, received it with good humour, and the conversation which followed gave a convincing proof, that religious motives were not so urgent, in behalf of her daughter's confinement, as those of private interest.' It seems that the officer's efforts were successful in saving the girl from the confined life of the convent, except that on investigation some of the convent life in the Azores was not as cloistered as others.

There were two nunneries on the island and, in contrast to the monasteries, these proved to be a great attraction, particularly for the junior officers. Johann Forster visited both nunneries and he described the clothing of the nuns:

> There are 2 Nunneries in this Town. Near the Matriz Parish Church is that of the order of Santa Clara, their Church is dedicated to San Joao. It consists of about 140 or 150 Nuns & as many Servants. The Nuns wear white Callico-cloth below & a kind of brown Serge-Cloak over it, & white coeffes, that are very singular. The next to them in a lower Situation of the hill, are the Nuns of Nossa Senhora de Concepcao, of which there are about 80 or 90 & as many Servants. These wear all white cloth & Cloaks, but on their breasts is fixed a blue silken orb with a silver plate – Image of Nossa Senhora . . .[6]

The Santa Clara convent housed about 150 nuns; they were colloquially called the 'black nuns' to differentiate them from their sisters who were clad only in white, with the image of the Virgin Mary on their bosoms. The white nuns were reckoned to be poorer and worse off than the black nuns. They were said to enter the convent in their later years, on account of poverty or other misfortune. The impressionable seventeen-year-old Elliott made a special mention of the nunnery as the place where he and his friends went every day; they spent hours chatting to two beautiful Spanish nuns through a grating provided for the purpose. George Forster paid only a single, short visit to see the white nuns, but like John Elliott he went with his friends from the ship to the so-called Black Convent three times:

Young and pleasant girls were mostly in the parlour or audience-room, with whom we exchanged presents through the double grating. They gave us delicious preserves in boxes, and we presented them with silk gloves, fans, lacquered boxes, flowers and similar Chinese trumpery, which they seemed to like. It should be noted that the width of the double iron grating was so great between us that we could barely reach out a pinch of snuff, or our gifts.[7]

Anders Sparrman, although he had left the ship by the time she reached Fayal, tells an anecdote of a Swedish ship at the Black Convent in Fayal. In spite of the separation of the grating, the sailors were able to dance with the nuns to the sounds of a barrel organ:

We were particularly welcome when we brought a superior hurdy-gurdy, with whose really fine notes a young handsome Swedish Orpheus appeared to tempt some of the nuns to forget their dreams of the high seat in the Kingdom of Heaven, the reward of their confinement behind walls and double gratings. On our side, we found we were no less roused by the hurdy-gurdy's throbbing and the susceptibility of the nuns; despite the heat of the climate we kept time in a dance with them.[8]

Conversation was very limited because of the language problems, and it had to be conducted through the grating. George Forster found the features of the black nuns very attractive and their complexions were fairer than he had expected. He noted:

Religion has not yet so entirely occupied their breast, as to extinguish every spark of corporeal fire; their eyes, which indeed were their finest features, still betrayed an attachment to nature; and if there is truth in the hundredth part of the accounts which we heard at Fayal, love reigns with absolute sway in the midst of their cloisters.[9]

Father and son agreed about their magnificent eyes and also their suppressed sexuality:

They have fine sparkling black Eyes, & often fine Teeth & very fine hands, are very slender in the waist, which we could see, when they threw their Cloaks back. They seem to be very amorous, in the spite of their Cloisters & double Grates. Their speech is very singing, & soft. If the Stories told us are true they are even very libidinous, & not being

able to satisfy their desires with Men, they endeavour to do it effectually
one way or other . . .[10]

We cannot help but notice that the sailors and the nuns had something
in common. Both vocations suffered the same frustrations through
being cooped up for too long with their own sex.

It was 19 July, the ship was fully provisioned for the last leg of her
journey and she sailed to the east with a favourable wind. It was an
uneventful passage and ten days later the Lizard was in sight. All
through the afternoon, they passed many ships plying to windward
and trying to get out of the English Channel. On the twenty-ninth,
Smeaton's lighthouse came into view on the Eddystone rock and later
the same day they landed at Plymouth. The next day, which was a
Sunday, the *Resolution* was anchored at Spithead. The great voyage had
at last come to an end. Later in the same day, Cook, with the artist
William Hodges, the astronomer William Wales and the two Forsters,
took the stagecoach from Portsmouth to London. They took with them
a young midshipman called Richard Grindall, who, after holding his
silence for three years, announced that he had married a young lady
just before he sailed from England. He had left her to join his ship only
an hour after the wedding ceremony.

In terms of historical importance, the voyage did not have the appeal
of the *Endeavour* voyage, when Australia and New Zealand, the two
largest landmasses in the South Pacific, had been accurately mapped
and charted. Some of the achievements of the *Resolution* were negative
rather than positive. In spite of his many months of endurance in sub-
zero temperatures, Cook did not discover the Antarctic continent. He
had quite deliberately followed up sightings and landfalls that had
already been discovered by earlier explorers and some of the work
had therefore been repetitive. But such negative comments fail to
appreciate the value and true purpose of the voyage. Antarctica apart,
there was no great landmass left to be discovered. The greatest
untouched land in the Pacific was New Caledonia, where Cook did in
fact land and chart one coast. As for the icy and forbidding continent
of Antarctica, he may not have set foot upon it but he proved its
existence beyond all reasonable doubt. He circumnavigated the Antarctic continent in almost every longitude, from the Indian Ocean to

the Pacific Ocean and on to the Atlantic. After a voyage of three years, he had lost only three men through accident and only one man through sickness. He penetrated south to an incredible 71°. He left England with the Dalrymple collection of Pacific voyages, which, without wishing to sound derogatory to Dalrymple, was full of vague positions, inaccurate longitudes and false sightings. After Cook's return, much of the Pacific was accurately mapped and charted, with coastal views and invaluable advice to future navigators. Most importantly, Cook came back with longitude calculations and accurate positions for a huge part of the southern Pacific, for which the astronomer William Wales must be given his due credit. The voyage, with its great forays into the Antarctic Circle, its two great sweeps through the Pacific islands, the charting of the New Hebrides and New Caledonia, the mapping of Tasmania and Tierra del Fuego, the discovery of South Georgia and the Sandwich Islands, was the longest voyage of discovery ever undertaken. To the connoisseur, it exceeded in many respects the voyage of the *Endeavour*. Cook brought back graphic pictures by William Hodges, accurate drawings by George Forster and, in spite of the difficult personality of his leading botanist, he brought back many new specimens carefully identified and catalogued by the Forsters.

It was high summer as they jolted through the lush green of the English countryside and the corn was ripening in anticipation of the harvest. What was it like to be travelling by land after three years at sea? What was the conversation in the stage as they rumbled along the dusty road to London? James Cook, one feels, must have been claustrophobic and uncomfortable on the stagecoach. The ship may have been crowded, but it was always possible to take the air and pace the quarterdeck. Did the travellers sit silently in this strange and yet familiar environment, on this, the last stage of their journey, each one of them absorbed in his own thoughts? They had been shipmates for over three years through thick and thin. Was there anything left which they had not already discussed with each other on the long and tedious parts of the voyage?

The voyage of the *Adventure* alone, with the rediscovery of Van Dieman's Land, was a worthy achievement in its own right, but it paled into insignificance alongside the voyage of the *Resolution*. The crew remembered the ice-edge cruise in the bitter cold of the Antarctic.

They remembered the dazzling display of the southern lights in the cold dark sky. They had seen the midnight sun inside the Antarctic Circle and they had seen the infinite expanse of the pack ice in the frozen southern seas. They had smiled together at young George Vancouver waving his hat from the end of the jib when their ship had travelled as far to the south as it was possible for man to go. The strange and mysterious statues of Easter Island had been studied and measured. The travellers had met the beautiful people of the Marquesas. The *Resolution* had cruised twice around the Society and the Friendly Islands, where the crew had enjoyed the welcome receptions and the emotional farewells. They had seen the South Sea paradise that was the Tonga Islands. The ship had been thrice to the unpredictable southern land of New Zealand, where their reception varied from the welcome at Dusky Sound and Queen Charlotte Sound to the massacre of Grass Cove. The *Resolution* had followed in the age-old footsteps of Mendana, Quiros, Torres and Tasman and had rediscovered and charted their long-forgotten islands. They had mapped and charted the New Hebrides to the fire and thunder of Nature unleashing her anger from the volcanoes. They had discovered the untouched people of New Caledonia and witnessed the uncontained joy of chief Teabooma when he was presented with his dog and bitch. They had sailed to the Isle of Pines and they had almost perished at sea in the process. The rounding of Cape Horn seemed tame by comparison with the terrible icy seas of the Antarctic. They had seen the icebergs being created from the desolate cliffs of South Georgia. Their wooden ship, driven by the wind alone, had sailed to some of the hottest places on the planet and they had sailed to the most bitterly cold seas. They had been where no man had been before. They had taken their ship as far as it was possible for a ship at the mercy of the elements to go.

It was time to report the findings to the Admiralty.

References

For convenience, references are given by the name of the author and the following abbreviations have been used. In the case of Burney, Clerk and Wales, the journals are published by the Hakluyt Society in the same volume as Cook's journal, edited by John Cawte Beaglehole. Single references are given explicitly.

Beaglehole: J. C. Beaglehole (ed.), *The Journals of Captain James Cook*, Hakluyt Society, Extra series no. XXXVII, vol. IV, *The Life of Captain James Cook*, 1974

Burney: James Burncy, *With Captain James Cook in the Antarctic and Pacific*, (ed.) Bcverley Hooper, Canberra, 1975

Cook: J. C. Beaglehole (ed.), *The Journals of Captain James Cook*, Hakluyt Society, Extra series no. XXXV, vol. II, *The voyage of the* Resolution *and* Adventure, 1961

Elliott: Christine Holmes (ed.), *Captain Cook's Second Voyage, The Journals of Lieutenants Elliot and Pickersgill*, London, 1984

G. Forster: George Forster, *A Voyage round the World, in his Brittanic Majesty's Sloop, the Resolution, commanded by Captain James Cook, during the years 1772–5* (2 vols), London, 1777

J. R. Forster: Michael E. Hoare (ed.), *The* Resolution *Journal of Johann Reinhold Forster*, Hakluyt Society, 2nd series, vols 151–5, 1982

Furneaux: J. C. Beaglehole (ed.), *The Journals of Captain James Cook*, pp.

729–45, Hakluyt Society, Extra series no. xxxv, vol. ii, *The Voyage of the* Resolution *and* Adventure, 1961

Rupert Furneaux, *Tobias Furneaux, circumnavigator*, London, 1960

Marra: John Marra, *Journal of the* Resolution's *voyage in 1772, 1773, 1774 and 1775*, London, 1775 (facsimile reprint: N. Israel, Amsterdam and New York, 1967)

Pickersgill: Christine Holmes (ed.), *Captain Cook's Second Voyage, The Journals of Lieutenants Elliot and Pickersgill*, London, 1984

Sparrman: Anders Sparrman, *A Voyage around the World with Captain James Cook in HMS* Resolution, London, 1944

Wales: J. C. Beaglehole (ed.), *The Journals of Captain James Cook*, pp. 776–869, Hakluyt Society, Extra series no. xxxv, vol. ii, *The Voyage of the* Resolution *and* Adventure, 1961

Notes

Preface
1 Sir Joseph Banks, *The Endeavour Journal of Joseph Banks*, ed. J. C. Beaglehole, 2 vols, Sydney, 1962.

One: London and Yorkshire
1 Lars E. Troide (ed.), *The Early Journals and Letters of Frances Burney*, vol. 1, 1768–1773, Oxford, 1988, p. 173.
2 Ibid.
3 Beaglehole, Cook to Hammond, 3 January 1772, p. 284.
4 J. Boswell, *The Life of Samuel Johnson*, LL.D., London, 1927, p. 435.
5 Ibid., p. 435.

Two: Resolution *and* Adventure
1 BM Add MS 27888, ff. 5–5v.
2 Ibid.
3 Cook, p. 9 n1.
4 J. R. Forster, ueber Georg Forster, *Annalen der Philosophie*, 1795.
5 J. R. Forster, p. 53.

6 Cook, Introduction, p. xx.
7 Ibid., p. xxi.
8 Ibid.
9 J. R. Forster, p. 128.
10 Allan Cunningham (1784–1842).

Three: Cape Town and Antarctica
1 Cook, p. 39, n1.
2 Ibid., p. 685.
3 Elliott, p. 11.
4 J. R. Forster, p. 181.
5 Lars E. Troide (ed.), *The Early Journals and Letters of Frances Burney*, vol. 1, 1768–1773, Oxford, 1988, p. 251.
6 J. R. Forster, p. 185.
7 Pickersgill, p. 63.
8 Sparrman, p. 21.
9 Ibid., p. 11.
10 Ibid., p. 12.
11 Cook, p. 80.
12 J. R. Forster, p. 233.

Four: The Rendezvous
1 G. Forster, vol. 1, p. 115.

2 Furneaux (Cook, p. 732).
3 Burney, p. 36.
4 Cook, p. 150 n1.
5 Burney, p. 38.
6 Ibid., p. 38.
7 Cook, p. 151 n1.
8 Sparrman, p. 25.
9 J. R. Forster, p. 248.
10 James Thomson (1700–48), *The Seasons* (1730).
11 Ibid., p. 271.
12 Ibid., p. 273.

Five: Tropical Interlude
1 Burney, p. 57.
2 Cook, p. 198.
3 Sparrman, p. 51.
4 Ibid., p. 49.
5 Wales (Cook, p. 796).
6 Cook, p. 216.
7 Sparrman, p. 78.
8 Ibid.
9 Pickersgill, p. 89.
10 Burney, p. 76.
11 Cook, p. 252.
12 J. R. Forster, p. 389.
13 Cook, p. 230 n4.

Six: To the Ends of the Earth
1 Sparrman, p. 101.
2 J. R. Forster, p. 429 n2.
3 Wales (Cook, p. 819).
4 Cook, p. 742 n1.
5 Ibid., p. 297 n2.
6 Burney (Cook, p. 750).
7 J. R. Forster, p. 438.
8 Elliott, p. 26.
9 J. R. Forster, p. 446.
10 Ibid., p. 444.
11 Cook, p. 323.

Seven: Following the Footsteps
1 J. R. Forster, p. 468.
2 Cook, p. 373.
3 Ibid., p. 430.
4 Ibid., p. 385.
5 Sparrman, p. 125.
6 Cook, p. 419 n1.
7 Wales (Cook, p. 842).

Eight: The New Hebrides
1 Cook, p. 444.
2 J. R. Forster, p. 544.
3 Ibid., p. 550.
4 G. Forster, vol. 2, p. 470.
5 Cook, p. 478.
6 J. R. Forster, p. 606.
7 Ibid.

Nine: New Caledonia
1 Wales (Cook, p. 864).
2 J. R. Forster, p. 646.
3 Wales (Cook, p. 867).
4 J. R. Forster, p. 654.
5 Cook, p. 551 n4.
6 Wales (Cook, p. xx).
7 Elliott, p. 35.
8 Ibid.
9 Cook, p. 580.
10 Ibid., p. 590.
11 J. R. Forster, p. 703.

Ten: The Atlantic
1 Cook, p. 621.
2 Ibid., p. 632 n4.
3 Ibid., p. 637.
4 J. R. Forster, p. 740.
5 Ibid., p. 757.
6 Ibid., p. 758.
7 G. Forster, vol. 2, p. 550.
8 Sparrman, p. 204.
9 G. Forster, vol. 2, p. xxx.
10 J. R. Forster, p. 759.

Index